THE KINGDOM ENTREPRENEUR

PARTNERING WITH GOD TO DOMINATE THE MARKETPLACE

DANITA HAYES

FOREWORD BY

LENIKA SCOTT

Enhanced
DNA
DEVELOP. NURTURE. ACHIEVE.
Publishing Division

Enhanced DNA Publishing

DenolaBurton@EnhancedDNA1.com

317-537-1438

The Kingdom Entrepreneur

Editor: Cynthia Roper

Cover Designer: Nicole Powell - NPInspired Design (www.npinspired.com)

Library of Congress Control Number: 2022909032

ISBN: 978-1-7369080-7-5

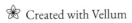 Created with Vellum

CONTENTS

PRAYER FOR YOU

Dear God, I thank You for choosing me as Your vessel to help inspire the person reading this book. I thank You that the person reading this book will accomplish the purpose and plan You have ordained for their life. I thank You that my story will light a fire in the person reading this book and they will grab the torch and run faster than ever. God, thank You for breakthroughs physically, financially, emotionally, and spiritually they will experience. Even as I share my story, I thank You, God, thank You for continued breakthroughs and healing on my behalf as well. In Jesus' name I pray. Thank God and Amen!

DEDICATION

This book is dedicated to my husband Chris Hayes and my children, Nadia, Nia, and Chris Jr. My family are the ones who have been there with me from day one. It has not just been my journey, but it has been OUR journey. They can relate and were there behind the scenes every day, through the good and the bad. My family is the greatest gift I have been blessed with and I thank God for them every day. I also want to acknowledge my Mother Carolyn Thomas-Clemons. She was my first teacher, and she taught me the most valuable lesson I have ever learned, which is how to pray. I also want to acknowledge all the people who have been with me through this journey for all the experiences that have brought me this far; both the good and bad ones. All the experiences were necessary for me to become the Kingdom Entrepreneur I am today.

FOREWORD

Foreword by Dr. Lenika Scott

I t was certainly an honor and privilege to be called upon to write this book foreword for Danita Hayes. Danita and I met as she was one of the faithful listeners of the Lifeline Prayer Ministry, a prayer assignment which birthed into a ministry in 2008. Her faithfulness to the line would soon elevate her to one of our co-hosts, as God would raise her up to lead and serve. We have been serving together for five years, as each week callers dial in to hear the gospel and receive prayer. Danita has been faithful to the call and such a joy to go to battle with.

Danita is a prophetic warrior and anointed vessel of the King who carries many gifts and wears different mantles- one being the mantle of wealth! Her wisdom and knowledge in real estate are strong. It has been such a joy to watch her grow and blossom. She is a business mogul on the rise, making great strides in the Kingdom. She is a woman of faith, and just as she stepped out on faith to launch her companies, she has stepped out on faith yet again obeying God to write this book!

Danita shares personal experiences about her spirit led journey in business, which will help guide others during their beginning steps. I am convinced more Kingdom Entrepreneurship literacy is needed as God is launching many to go forth and take ownership of the business mountain. This book is necessary and a must read! It sheds light to the significance of the timing of GOD in business, but most importantly, it highlights that it is imperative you follow His leading every step of the way.

Two of my favorite lines from the book are :

"Kingdom entrepreneurs do not work for themselves; they work for God."

"I believe it is a prerequisite for Kingdom Entrepreneurs to spend a lot of time with God and completely surrender to Him."

This book is for anyone who desires to see CHANGE.

If you are stagnant and stuck in your business, this book is for you!

If you need help and wisdom as you navigate through the entrepreneurship space "God's way" this book is for you!

Also included are Danita's list of personal daily affirmations aligning with the word of God, which readers can take and use. These affirmations cover every area of your life. Say them daily over yourself. When you declare God's word over your life,

Heaven has to respond. After reading this book, there will be a greater sense of knowing that God chose YOU! Fortunately, if you are holding this book in your hands, it is no mistake. Kingdom Entrepreneurship is not an *easy feat,* but if He called you to walk this path, He will give you the grace, the strength, and the tenacity to carry it out!

Prophetess Lenika Scott

--

INTRODUCTION

When I first began to write this book, I did not know where or how to start. After speaking to several individuals who had written books, they said, "Get a notebook and just start writing." God has been pressing upon my spirit to write this book for a while now. I never aspired to be an author, so I know this is something that came from Him. I pray what I have to say will inspire someone who was once just like me, trying to find their way. I pray my story and my testimony will encourage someone to keep going. Initially, I struggled with what I should share, and what I thought might be too much information. Well, God revealed to me what I have inside of me and what I have to say could help someone else reach their next level, and I should not be ashamed of what I have gone through to get to this point. He has shown me I am right where I am supposed to be at this time in my life, and I think this book will help you realize you too are right where you are supposed to be as well. Once I received the revelation that God created me with everything I needed to be successful, and He already knew ahead of time the obstacles I would encounter; these obstacles were necessary for me to be prepared, equipped, and processed for where He is taking me and where I am going.

I am sharing this story because I believe it will help encourage someone who may be in a type of financial situation right now. I hope this story will encourage you to realize you, too can go from a negative bank account to owning multiple successful businesses.

It was a Sunday afternoon around 4:30pm and I dropped my son off at a birthday party. I had about 2 hours to kill before picking him up at 6:30pm. I did not want to drive all the way back home because the distance from my home to the party was about 30 minutes. I knew by the time I got home and sat down, it would be time for me to go back and pick him up. I was in an area where there were plenty of stores for shopping and restaurants to eat. I could have easily spent a good two hours; however, my bank account was overdrawn, and I only had about $5.00 cash in my purse. I will never forget this time in my life. This was a time where I was struggling financially and was literally putting every-thing I had into building my business. So, with that being said, shopping or eating out for those two hours was not even some-thing I could do if I wanted to.

I heard the Holy Spirit say, "Go to the store and buy a 5-subject notebook. You will spend the time waiting for your son to start writing a book." I am thinking that is a great idea. I can sit in my car where it is quiet, gather my thoughts, and begin to write.

I walk into the store and go to the notebook section. I am looking at the 5-subject notebooks and noticing that they are all around $4.99 and I only had $5.00 in my purse literally. Even if I would have gotten the $4.99 notebook, I had no extra change for tax. So, instead of picking up the 5-subject notebook, I got the one subject notebook that was only $2.99. I remember laughing to myself, "Now that is in my price range." I took the notebook to the register to pay,and the cashier rang it up. She looks at the notebook and then she picks one up from behind the counter, and it is a 5-subject notebook. She said, "Would you like to get this one for only fifty cents?" She said, "It is way cheaper and you get 5 subjects instead of one." I said, "Absolutely!!" I ended up paying fifty-three cents for the 5-subject notebook. Not only was it the 5-subject notebook the Holy Spirit initially wanted me to get, but it was also my favorite color, which is red. I know many may not think this is a big deal, but to me it was confirmation God wanted me to write this book, and that He would guide my every footstep in getting it done. He also showed me He was my provider, and He would make sure I have everything I needed along this entre-preneurship journey. He showed me He would order my steps and take care of every little detail, even down to my favorite color. I see God in everything, and I look for Him everywhere. I named this book "The Kingdom Entrepreneur" because that is who I am.

My definition of a Kingdom Entrepreneur is: One who has been chosen by God to thrive in the marketplace and who completely surrenders his or her own will over to the will of God. One who seeks instructions daily from God and obeys the instructions regardless of how difficult or out of the ordinary they may be. One who ultimately understands that their successes are not for them to be glorified, but for their Father in Heaven to be glorified, which in turn draws more souls to the Kingdom.

As you read this book, you will experience my journey as a Kingdom Entrepreneur. The amazing thing about Kingdom Entrepreneurship is God will always use your successes and your journey for Him to get the Glory. As a Kingdom Entrepreneur, you are not the boss... God is!

Do Not Abort The Mission

God gave me a prophetic dream around the time I really began to start my real estate company. This dream was the catalyst to setting a fire under me not to quit and to keep pushing, no matter how hard it was. In the dream, I was sitting in a boardroom with a lot of women. I was sitting at the head of the table and one by one, each of the women came up to me and told me they were excited because they were pregnant. There was also another group of women waiting outside of the boardroom and they were talking. The women who were excited about being pregnant walked out of the boardroom one by one and spoke with the women outside of the boardroom. After they would speak to those women, they would come back one by one and tell me they have decided to get an abortion. I was telling the women, "No, do not get an abortion. You were so excited about being pregnant. Why did you change your mind?" I woke up, and I heard the spirit of the Lord say, "Do Not Abort The Mission."

I instantly received the interpretation of this dream when I woke up. What God revealed is that I was being called to inspire, uplift, motivate, and encourage other women to birth the vision and the mission God had given them. He also showed me no matter how hard things may get, I must not abort the mission and I must encourage others not to. If you are reading this book, the dream was meant for you as well. He also showed me many will get side-tracked and, by getting connected with the wrong people, may be convinced to abort the mission. The women outside the board-room were convincing those inside to get abortions. They were outside of the boardroom because they were outside of the Will of God. Being outside the Will of God is the most dangerous place to be. There is no promotion outside of His will and, most importantly, there is no protection outside of His Will. It is also dangerous to be connected with people who are outside of His Will. They can attach themselves to you and your destiny and cause you to miss out on what God has for you. This dream was full of wisdom nuggets, and it was also confirmation of what God called me to. This dream was the catalyst to the beginning of my Kingdom Entrepreneurship journey. God speaks to us through our dreams, and it is very important we pay attention to them and pray for His revelation and interpretation of them.

The bible verse I am reminded of as I am typing out this dream is Matthew 5:14-16, and it reads, "You are the light of the world-like a city on a hilltop that cannot be hidden. No one lights a lamp and then puts it under a basket. Instead, a lamp is placed on a stand where it gives light to everyone in the house. In the same way, let your good deeds shine out for all to see, so everyone will praise your heavenly Father." God wants us to shine and shine brightly in the marketplace. We are the light of the world. Never be afraid to exhibit the gifts, talents, and abilities God has placed inside of you. Your gifts are not just for you but are meant to inspire others to shine as well. Someone right now is waiting on you to shine so they can shine, too.

How Did I Get Here?

I am certainly not the same person who used to be afraid to open her mouth and say what needs to be said. I am certainly not the same person who would be so nervous to speak publicly I would get nauseous, and my voice would tremble as I spoke. Looking back, where did this newfound confidence and boldness come from? Who does she think she is to open and run multiple businesses, travel the country speaking in front of large crowds, telling her story and inspiring others? Who told her she was good enough? Who told her she was smart enough? Who told her she was fearless, and she had the power within to do these things? As a Kingdom Entrepreneur, all of my confidence came from God. I finally figured it out. I figured out the key to my destiny and the key to my success. I figured out who I was, and everything the enemy tried to accomplish in my life from childhood until now would not prosper because I figured out who God says I am. I began to understand I was a child of the Most High

God. He showed me who I was when I became intentional about getting to know Him. There was a time in my life when God was drawing me closer to Him and calling me higher in the things of God. I have always had a relationship with Him, but during this time I was really feeling an extreme closeness to Him. So close I could feel His presence and, most importantly, I could hear His voice and know it was Him. During this time in my life, my husband and I were having financial problems. In the past, I was always able to depend on my husband to fix everything, no matter what the situation was. Unfortunately, this time, he was not able to. In this season, God did not allow him to fix it. God was showing us both at the time that we needed to solely depend on God and tap into the source. This had to happen because God was molding me and preparing me to understand that He is my source. He wanted me to seek Him like never before, and to trust HIM with every fiber of my being. It was a necessary process for where He was taking me. He stripped me of everything. I lost some close relationships with friends and family members. I went from working for a real estate company, which provided me with security, to opening my own real estate company. It was frightening to start over and build something new alone. During this time in my life, God had me in a season of isolation so I could learn to hear God's voice above anyone else's and not be afraid to obey His voice regardless of what others may think.

There would be times in the middle of the night I would feel my bed gently shaking. I would wake up and look over at my husband to see if he felt it too, but he would be sound asleep. It never frightened me because I always felt a sweet angelic presence and had an inner knowing it was Angels waking me up to pray. For a while, this would happen almost every night. When it happened, I would get up, go to my prayer closet, and spend the most intimate times with God. I would talk to Him, and He would talk to me. During this time of prayer, I literally felt my spirit connecting with the spirit of God. These were the times God would show me visions, give me ideas, and most importantly, spiritual downloads which helped me grow in Christ. I was so hungry for time with God some nights I would pray for hours and wake up in the morning in my prayer closet. As I focused more on Him, doors opened for me in my business and in ministry. The Word tells us in Matthew 6:33, "If we seek ye first the kingdom of God and His righteousness, all these other things will be added unto you." God already had a plan for my life, and He knew the outcome. It was up to me to decide to seek Him for direction and guidance so I could walk the plan out. I am grateful and thankful for what He has done in my life and what He is continuing to do. He still has more for me, and I will continue to seek Him daily to make sure I am walking in the Will of God.

When the Angels would come and wake me up to pray, it was truly an awesome experience, which built my faith like never before. Later, when I connected with my prayer sister, Lenika Scott, she told me about the visions God showed her of Angels waking people up in the middle of the night. I was in awe of God's power and definitely knew it was confirmation of what I had been experiencing. Whenever you are awakened in the middle of the night for no apparent reason, I believe it is God calling you to spend time with Him and pray. I truly believe in these special moments with God, miracles are birthed, and the supernatural is being poured into your life. The true key to success is allowing the spirit of God to become one with yours. John 7:37-39(NLT) comes to mind, "On the last day, the climax of the festival Jesus stood and shouted to the crowds, 'Anyone who is thirsty may come to me! Anyone who believes in me may come and drink! For the scriptures declare; Rivers of living water will flow from his heart.'" (When He said, "living water," He was speaking of the Spirit who would be given to everyone believing in Him. But the spirit had not yet been given because Jesus had not yet entered into His glory.)." This bible verse tells us several things.

1. The rivers of living water flow forever because they are living. The rivers of living water are the spirit of God.

2. We now have complete access to His spirit to become one with ours because He is no longer on the earth and His glory has been revealed. So, if we believe, we can continuously have His spirit flow through us.

3. As we submerge ourselves in the rivers of living water, we automatically activate the supernatural in our lives. In doing so, we can accomplish anything God has called us to because we are no longer operating in our own strength, but with the strength of God.

Also, remember where the spirit of God is, there is liberty, peace, joy, wisdom, knowledge, favor, healing, provision, and anything else you may need. The list of who He is and what His presence embodies could go on and on.

The most amazing thing about this is God will freely pour out His spirit on whoever wants to receive; all we have to do is ask. God is not a respecter of persons and if He can show Himself mighty for me, He will do it for you, too. During this time, God was showing me that during my journey as an entrepreneur, He would send assistance for me to carry out the vision. This was a time when I was really getting to know who God was.

Let us take a close look at who God really is and start by looking at the definition of God. According to the Oxford dictionary, God is: "The creator and ruler of the universe and source of all moral authority; the supreme being." God has different names in the bible and each one has a meaning:

Elohim (God)

Yahweh (Lord Jehovah)

El Elyon (The Most High)

Adonai (Lord, Master)

El Shaddai (Lord God Almighty)

El Olam (The Everlasting God)

Jehovah Jireh (The Lord will provide)

Jehovah Rapha (The Lord Who Heals You)

Jehovah Nissi (The Lord is My Banner)

El Qanna (Jealous God)

Jehovah Mekoddishkem (The Lord Who Sanctifies You)

Jehovah Shalom (The Lord is Peace)

Jehovah Sabaoth (The Lord of Hosts)

Jehovah Raah (The Lord is My Shepherd)

Jehovah Tsidkenu (The Lord Our Righteousness)

Jehovah Shammah (The Lord is There)

I Am (The God of Everything)

The name says it all. His name is above all names and His name encompasses everything we need to do all He has called us to do, and to be everything He intended for us to be. To be a Kingdom Entrepreneur, we must first recognize who He is. When we know who He is, He will then reveal to us who we are.

When you read the Bible, you will see many instances where God changes someone's name to the name of what their future looks like; not what their current circumstances are. He will always reveal to you who you are by what He calls you. If you remember, God changed Abram's name to Abraham, which means, "Father of Many Nations". At the time, Abram did not have any children. As a matter of fact, he was 99 years old. He and his wife were at an age where physically it would be impossible for them to conceive a child. God showed Abraham what his future looked like by changing his name. Your name is a representation of who you are. The first question anyone asks you when they meet you is, "What is your name?" Your name is the first thing people associate with who you are. God knows the importance of calling someone a name that represents where they are going instead of where they currently are. He revealed to Abraham who He was by changing his name to what his future looked like. So, every time someone called his name, they were basically calling out to him "Father of Many Nations". This was being spoken over Abraham daily until it became a reality.

Once we have accepted Christ into our lives, He changes our names, too.

According to God's word we are known as a child of the King, heirs of His Kingdom, royalty, friends of God, the lenders and not the borrowers, above and not beneath. We are joined to the Lord, and we are one spirit with Him. We also now have the mind of Christ, and the list goes on.

The day I decided to intentionally seek Him was the day my life changed. God showed me who He was in my life and then He revealed to me who I was. Your identity is critical in your entrepreneurship journey. Entrepreneurs are leaders by nature and, more often than not, will be the first to do a thing. Being the first to do something comes with a lot of pressure and push back. If you are reading this book and you are an entrepreneur, you know exactly what I am talking about. When you are confident in who you are, and the vision you have been given by God to do what He has called you to, you will be able to overcome any obstacle that may come your way. Knowing who you are and what you have been called to do is the one factor which keeps you going when times get tough.

Oftentimes I look back at my life and wonder what made me to be the person I have become. How we were raised, and our environment, is what initially molds us into the people we are. When we are children, we do not have a choice about our environment or how we are raised, but once we become adults, we now have the power to change whatever we want in our lives if we are willing to do the work. It is called personal development. Personal development is a mandatory component when it comes to entrepreneurship. Have you ever noticed successful entrepreneurs are constantly reading books, taking classes, listening to inspirational messages, and constantly investing in themselves? Why? Because they understand the importance of constantly evolving. If you have not changed at all over a span of time, then you have not grown. Even though we all reach the age of 18, where we are considered to be an adult, it does not mean we stop growing. There is no cap on your growth and what levels you can grow mentally. As a leader, you should want to intentionally grow and go to higher levels, mentally and spiritually.

It takes years for children to learn certain behaviors and for their minds to be conditioned to believe the lessons taught. As adults, if we want something different or want change, it will also take time to unlearn hindering patterns and habits. It takes time to reprogram your mind to a new way of thinking. The decision to transform yourself and adopt a new mindset is yours. I know sometimes it takes a while for us to even recognize the things in us need change. We get to a point in our lives where we notice certain cycles and patterns. These patterns are clues something is wrong. For me, I noticed a cycle in myself where I would start something and not finish. I would get excited about an idea, get started, lose interest, and just let it go all together. This was an area of my life I had to bring before God and ask for help. Through prayer, God showed me He would not allow me to go to the next level in anything until I became focused and finished what I started. Unfinished assignments will lead to a path of stagnation and frustration. He showed me He could not trust me to go to the next level if I had not mastered my current level. All of this makes perfect sense, but for some reason, I kept falling into these same patterns. This pattern was keeping me stuck, and I was not growing.

Another example is choosing the wrong people to get involved in relationships with or having a hard time managing your money. I do not know about you, but I have experienced all these examples in my life. The one thing we must understand is these patterns are just symptoms of the root cause. As you know, with physical sickness in our bodies, we will experience symptoms derived from the root illness. For instance, if my blood pressure is too high, I may experience a headache, blurred vision or even dizziness. I can take something for my headache, but it still does not heal the root cause, which is high blood pressure. To heal the high blood pressure, it is going to take a little more than just taking a pill. I may have to change my eating habits and exercise daily to heal the root cause. By doing these things, I will not see an immediate change on the first day, but if I am consistent, I will see a change over time. If I decide to go the route of healing myself naturally, the process will take much longer before I see the results. So, as you can see, the symptoms are the headache, blurred vision, and dizziness, but the cause of these symptoms is the root illness, which is high blood pressure. This same ideology can apply to our mental wellness. The symptoms are the patterns and cycles and more often than not the root illness or sickness is some type of trauma or past hurt which has not been dealt with. Many are dealing with things from their childhood that were swept under a rug and never dealt with or even some things that happened as adults. These things will always resurface themselves in some way. You may experience them in your finances, your relationships, the way you do business, and even in how you may raise your children.

When I think back to my childhood and how we were raised in a single-parent household and not always having the things we needed, it helped me to understand why and how I became accustomed to a poverty mindset. Because of what we saw in our environment, living in lack is what seemed normal to us. So, even as adults when we were able to do better for ourselves financially, we still had the same mentality, which caused us to continue to live in poverty.

It does not matter how much money you make, what matters is if you know how to manage the money you have. The key Kingdom Principle I was not utilizing at the time was sowing and reaping. Did you know one of the key components to getting out of poverty is to give? I know it sounds crazy, but it is a Kingdom Principle, and it is how God set up the Kingdom. When you are a giver, God will always make sure you have more to give. Logically, you would think that you should hold on to what you have, especially if you do not have much; however, when you do this, you are not preparing room to increase the capacity for the level that God wants to bless you on. The more we give, the more God gives back to us. Let us look at these Bible verses to back up this very important Kingdom Principle. 2 Corinthians 9:6, "Now this I say, he who sows sparingly, will also reap sparingly, and he who sows bountifully will also reap bountifully." What does this mean, "The way you give will be the way you receive," 2 Corinthians 9:10. I kept finding myself falling into this same pattern of never having enough money, no matter how much money I made. I fell into this same pattern and cycle because I was not being a good steward of what God gave me. I was not tithing or sowing consistently. Doing these things consistently is also a part of being a good steward over your finances. Many times, the areas in your life you are constantly bound by are more than likely the areas God has called you to to help set others free or if there is something that really bothers you and you want to see change, that too is an area you have been called to to be a change-maker.

What I have learned is that more often than not, when we meet people with some type of character flaw a lot of times, the flaw is there because no one has ever challenged it or they have never dealt with a past issue, myself included. I remember for a long time, I dealt with the spirit of pride. I felt as though I could do everything myself and did not ask for help, even if I needed it. What God began to show me in my entrepreneurship journey was that I would need people to help me. I would need people who I could talk to for advice, and I would have to be willing to listen and learn. One day I had to really self-reflect and ask myself why am I this way. As I began to really dig deep, I started to realize I felt as a woman, that I had something to prove. I felt I needed to accomplish things on my own so no one else could take credit for what I accomplished. God quickly reminded me He would get the glory for anything I ever thought I had accomplished and to remember it is Him who gives us the power to do all things through Christ who strengthens us.

Although He reminded me that He gets the glory, I still had to dig deeper to ask myself why I felt this way. I think many black women can relate to feeling as though they are invisible or not given the respect they deserve. For many years, people have looked down on us and assumed the worst about us. Even as time has evolved, and we have accomplished so many amazing things despite the constant resistance in society we are forced to reckon with. We still fight to be heard and valued. I grew up in a family of 5. I had two older siblings and two younger. For the first 8 years of my life, I was the youngest and had two older brothers. We fought like cats and dogs sometimes like most siblings do. The dynamic of our family, with me being the youngest at the time and the only girl, plays a huge role in my personality today.

Even at that young age, I always had my own opinions and was very independent. I remember when I was about 4 or 5 years old, I wanted to go outside and play with my friends. My mom would make my older brother come with me everywhere I went. I remember one day he was walking me outside to play and he had his arm around me like a big brother would do to protect his little sister and I pushed his arm off of me.

At the time I was thinking, 'I am a big girl and I do not need my brother watching me while I am playing outside with my friends.' I remember before leaving the house with him, I told my mom I could go outside by myself, and she said, "No, your brother is coming with you." I can laugh now because I know I was a feisty little thing trying to be independent at the age of 4 or 5.

This dynamic in my household was what I contended with as a child, constantly proving my independence against my two older brothers. When I finally dug deep and went all the way back to childhood, this was how I was able to recognize certain triggers in my adult life which would cause me to become angry with people when I felt I was not being heard or was being disrespected. I realized those experiences as a child are what birthed the spirit of pride. The feeling where I needed to prove something to people, and I could do everything alone. The spirit of pride is a one-way ticket to stagnation. Everyone wants to be heard and valued, but for me I believe the pride I was dealing with stemmed from the dynamic of being the youngest and only girl at that time and not being heard. Now that I recognize what it is, I can understand where the symptoms came from and work on the root problem. Once I really became intentional about my prayer life and seeking God, He really showed me these things about myself through prayer. When I pray, God shows me things through visions.

One particular morning, as I prayed, I saw a vision of a heart. It was a fake heart, the kind we normally see on Valentine's Day. As I watched the heart beating inside of my body, I saw the hand of God peeling back layers of the fake heart until He got to the core, my real heart, which now looked like a real human heart. Then I saw Him covering the real heart with His hands and my body began to illuminate from the inside out. What the Holy Spirit revealed to me that day is God was healing me from the inside out so God's Glory could be revealed through my life. He showed me it was no longer me, but Him operating through me. The dream is what will happen in our lives if we allow God to pull back the layers of our hearts so He can heal us completely from the inside out.

If you can understand how the natural heart functions and its importance to make sure the entire body functions properly, you will be able to understand the importance of our spiritual hearts and how it is the root of everything inside of us. Here is a quick lesson on the natural heart. The heart is a pump that squeezes and pushes out blood through blood vessels and provides every cell in the body with oxygen and nutrients. EVERY cell in the body is affected by the heart's function. This is why when you see people with heart problems, other organs and other functions of the body start to fail, but the root cause is the heart. Just as our natural hearts determine the overall health and functions of our physical bodies, our spiritual hearts do the same for our spirits. In order for God's Glory to freely flow through you and for you to do all God has called you to, there can be no blockages of the heart. Blockages such as :

Hate

Envy

Jealousy

Unforgiveness

Depression

Laziness

Procrastination

Disobedience

Idolatry

Pride

Remember, any of these blockages will hinder the flow of God's Glory in your life.

All the pride and past hurts I was dealing with, day by day as I intentionally prayed, He removed layer after layer until I was set free. He reminded me He would set up divine connections for me to get the help I needed and I had to be open to receiving help. He broke the spirit of pride off me so I could elevate to my next level. God quickly promoted me in the natural realm because I handled some things in the spirit realm first. I went from barely being able to pay my bills to making a high six-figure salary, all in a matter of 2 years. Kingdom entrepreneurs handle things in the spirit before seeing an earthly manifestation. In other words, with every single thing we do in our business, we consult God first in prayer.

Another issue with being prideful is if you have no one around you... you have no one to check you. What we do not realize is the partnerships and relationships we have in our lives force us to become a better version of ourselves. This is true because, by default, we have someone who will hold us accountable when we do not do it for ourselves. We are all working on ourselves constantly. It is a choice we make and become intentional about when we really want to change. There should come a time in your life where you self-reflect and take inventory of your life. Look around you, look at your environment, your relationships, your bank account, your business, or careers and really ask yourself, am I content with where I am in every area of my life right now? If the answer is no, then it is time to make a decision to be intentional about transforming your life. If you take this self-inventory and after asking the question you are content with where you are, then first be thankful for where you are and, secondly, become intentional about moving to your next level.

Regardless of where you are in your life, it all starts with you making a decision to be intentional about becoming a better you.

This means you can no longer place blame on anything or anyone from what may have happened in the past or during your childhood. If you need healing, get healed. Things not dealt with from your past will hinder you in the future. Many wonder why they can only get so far and then hit a wall. Unfortunately, they do not realize many of the things in our past we have held onto can cause us to get stuck and prevent us from growing to the levels God has for us. I know it can be frustrating because I have been there. I was stuck and stagnant because I had not made the decision to deal with my issues and become a better me.

I was dealing with pride, unforgiveness, and not being able to trust people; I had a few instances where a handful of people betrayed me. My willingness to not forgive was only hurting me and holding me back. I had to learn how to separate the person's behavior from the person. It was not the person; it was the spirit dwelling in the person. The Word of God tells us we are never fighting with flesh and blood, it is the spirit we are warring with. With that being said, we have to learn how to separate the two and realize the best way to fight those battles is on your knees praying to God.

Once I was able to deal with these issues, I was able to operate in my gifts freely. I was able to grow as a person, which in turn helped me to grow my business. When I decided to desperately seek God for answers and wisdom, He began to transform me. I believe a prerequisite for Kingdom Entrepreneurs is to spend a lot of time with God and completely surrender to Him. After all, your main goal as a Kingdom Entrepreneur is to help build the Kingdom through marketplace ministry and to finance Kingdom projects. Kingdom Entrepreneurs do not work for themselves, they work for God.

I began to see that unless I changed my perspectives and transformed my mind, I would never reach the levels I desired or the levels God had for me. So, to answer the question, How did I get here... first, I had to recognize the things in me that needed to be changed. Secondly, I had to sincerely bring those things before God and truly repent. The true meaning of repentance is "Responding to God's love by being transformed in your convictions and actions. It means turning toward God and away from whatever dishonors Him. Biblical repentance is not about your emotions, your sin, your efforts, or your resolve. It's about your surrender." (christianparenting. com) Basically when you decide to repent and surrender, God can then use you in mighty ways because His will becomes your will. He will take you places you never thought were possible. The day I completely surrendered to God was the day it all began. God downloaded the revelation of His Word and revealed to me who I was in Him. Once you truly learn who you are and whose you are, you can accomplish anything. These are some of the affirmations I say daily. I have accumulated them over the years straight from God's Word. I say them out loud every day because I truly believe our words have power, and we create our destinies with the words we speak.

I declare:

The Lord is my Shepherd I shall not want

I have the mind of Christ.

I am the head and not the tail.

I am above and not beneath.

I am chosen by God.

My God shall supply all my needs according to His riches in Glory.

Wealth and riches shall live in my house.

I am fearfully and wonderfully made.

I am royalty because I am a child of God.

No weapon formed against me shall prosper, and every tongue that rises against me shall be condemned.

I dwell in the secret place of the Most High and no plague shall come nigh my dwelling.

By His stripes I am healed.

All these affirmations cover every area of your life. Say these daily over yourself. When you declare God's Word over your life, Heaven has to respond.

THE PROCESS IS
NECESSARY

L
ike many in the African American community, many of us have similar stories growing up. Where I was from, it was very rare we saw our friends grow up in a two-parent household. My siblings and I were no exception. I am the middle child of my mother's five children three boys and two girls. My parents divorced when I was five years old. My mother did what most single mothers did back then and that was to work hard and take care of her kids. There were times I came home from school, and we had no electricity or no phone and sometimes no food. My mother worked hard to keep us out of public housing, but in doing so... she really could not afford most of the necessities needed to keep up our household. We heated our home with kerosene heaters and sometimes we either had to take cold showers or heat large pots of water to take baths. There were even times when our water would get cut off and we would have to go to our grandparent's house to take baths and fill up large jugs of water to

take back to the house. So, when I tell you I know what it is like to live in poverty, I truly understand. Growing up in this type of environment is the recipe for repeating a generational curse for poverty.

Although we had this type of thing going on at home, my mother's faith was very strong. She kept us in church all the time and always taught us about God. As a kid, being in church all the time was not fun, but I am thankful now my mom stood her ground with us. We could not always do what everyone else was doing because my mom would not allow it. I was always upset about it back then, but my firm upbringing kept me out of a lot of unhealthy situations and environments. I definitely had my share of sneaking around as a teenager, but for the most part, my mom kept a tight rein on me. I have always known that I wanted more and could never get accustomed to living this type of life once I became an adult.

Often people will accept their environments and cannot see past them. I am an avid believer in being intentional about getting out of your environment to see beyond what you currently see. One thing my mom did with us growing up was to drive to neighborhoods with really nice houses just for us to look at. I do not know if she realized the major impact this small act of driving around these neighborhoods had on me and my life. It gave me the capacity and the ability to dream for more and go beyond what my current circumstances were. What I learned is it is important to expose yourself to new experiences, which will continue to fuel your mind to dream big. My mom exposed us to as much as she could so we could have a vision of where we wanted to go in life. I even remember one time my mother brought a small jar of caviar home for us to taste. She said it is good to try new foods and learn different cultures, so we are not ignorant to certain things when we get out in the real world.

Remember your surroundings, environment, and the people around you matter. Be intentional about exposing yourself to big things. Once you have seen something big, you cannot unsee it. If you cannot unsee it, then it's inevitable your mind will develop the capacity to dream bigger than where you are right now. This reminds me of Romans 12:2(KJV) which says, " And be not conformed to this world: but be ye transformed by the renewing of your mind, that ye may prove what is that good, and acceptable, and perfect, will of God."

In this Bible verse, it reminds us not to conform to our surroundings. It tells us we should be intentional about consistently renewing our minds with the word of God. In doing so, we will become transformed.

My grandparents played a major role in helping my mom with us. My grandmother was our babysitter and watched us during the summer when we were out of school and my mom had to work. My grandfather definitely stood in the gap for my dad. He was the only father figure we had, and he was a good one. Yes, my parents had their issues with each other, but the biggest obstacle that kept my dad from us was his mental illness. My dad and I were very close when I was a little girl, but when he became sick, we rarely got to see him anymore. I can vividly remember the day my mom received a phone call my dad was being admitted to a mental hospital, I believe I was 8- years- old. The news devastated me, and

I felt heartbroken. As a child, this was something heavy to deal with. I missed him so much it hurt. I also had a fear of thinking when I grew up, I would be in a mental hospital as well. This was something I contended with as a child and never really understood what mental illness was and how people were affected by it. As I got older and did more research on mental illness, I found it could be hereditary, so of course in the back of my mind, I always thought about that.

We all know in the black community, mental illness is not something people discuss openly or will admit they have. I did not see my father again until I was a senior in high school. He seemed to be doing better. He had his own place and would come and see me sometimes. He was able to come to my graduation, and I was very happy and proud to have him there. We stayed in touch throughout my college years, but lost touch again. When I became an adult, we reconnected again, and the relationship has been off and on because of his illness. I certainly do not blame him at all. Now, as an adult, I understand what his capabilities and capacities were due to his illness.

I give you this glimpse into my childhood so you can see what has molded me and shaped me into the person I am today. I believe we never go through things in vain. Everything we go through in our lives, especially in our childhood, builds our character and forms our opinions of who we are. Looking back at my childhood and the things I have gone through, I choose to use those things to learn, grow and move forward. We can actually miss out on the blessings of God because we choose to dwell on the past. We can easily miss what God is trying to do in our lives if we do not take the things we have gone through and ask God, "What are You trying to teach me in this situation and what purpose does this situation serve in my life?" If we learn to focus on the lesson and not the circumstance, it will open doors for promotion in all areas of our lives.

Growing up in our household, my mother was a real woman of God. I always say the most valuable gift my mom has ever given me was to teach me how to pray and to pray often. Every morning, my mother gathered us together, and we prayed together as a family. She was making sure she sent her kids out into the world equipped and protected from the things we see and from the things we cannot see. My mom made us say the Lord's Prayer, Psalm 91, Psalm 23, and 2 Peter 2: 24 (a healing scripture), every morning. She covered us every morning, even when we had an attitude and did not want to pray. I am so glad she never wavered from her faith, even when times got tough. I saw my mom work hard to provide for us. I never saw her turn away from God, even when things did not work out the way we thought it should. She was my first role model and still is. I still watch how she handles situations even though I am an adult now. I am still learning and gleaning from her. Prayer was always a big part of my life. I never really understood until I became an adult how important prayer really was, until I realized when we pray, we are actually pulling those things down from Heaven that rightfully belong to us as God's children. Prayer activates your destiny and God's plan for your life here on earth. Prayer gives us a huge advantage over those who do not pray, because when we pray, we are coming into alignment with what has already been done. We are coming into agreement with it by speaking it out into the atmosphere and pulling it into the earthly realm. Before it happens on earth, it has to happen in the spiritual realm first. When we pray God gives us instructions, He shows us what is next and keeps us one step ahead. When prayer is consistent in your life, results become the norm.

What I have learned is that if you do not know your destination, you will not understand your journey. It really was not until I became an entrepreneur and became serious about my relationship with God I realized why God had taken me through all the things I had gone through prior. I understood God uses every situation, every trial, all the good and the bad to equip us with the tools we need for our destination. You may think things are not going your way and the whole time, God is working it out for your good. Romans 8:28 says, "All things work together for the good for those who love the Lord and are called according to His purpose." Guess what, Kingdom Entrepreneur you are called according to His purpose, so by default, ALL things are working out in your favor.

God is the only one who can tell you where you are going and how you will get there. One day while I was praying, God showed me a vision of myself speaking in front of a large crowd of people. This was right before I started my real estate company and began working for myself full-time. I was baffled by what I saw because I was far from being a public speaker and had absolutely no desire to be one. He showed me the vision but did not show me how I was going to get to that stage. Little did I know at the time my entrepreneurship journey would be the reason I would be on that stage. I have been on many stages after God showed me the vision.

It did not happen right away because He had to process me before I would be ready to hit the stage.

The processing of a person is always necessary. God will never elevate you to levels you are not properly prepared for. We can get frustrated during the processing stages of our journey. I know when God was preparing me and processing me I had to go through some hard times, uncomfortable times, and some alone times. Let's talk about being alone. I know I am not the only entrepreneur God took through a period of isolation. A time where your family and friends sort of fell off, and it was just you. I experienced this time where I had no one to depend on but God. This was a time where many of my close friendships were changing, and my husband and I were struggling financially. This was a time where I had no choice but to trust God. This was a time where I would literally sit in the presence of God for hours and pray. This was a time where I totally tapped into His presence and God showed me the way. I recall taking a journal into my prayer closet with me as I prayed, and God would give me ideas and strategies to build my business. Everything God gave me to do required me to come outside of my comfort zone. Obedience was the key ingredient to my success. God will give many a vision of what He wants them to do, and only those who are obedient in executing the vision will see the promise. When God gives you a vision to execute, no one else will understand the vision like you do. I understand the excitement and how you want to share it with others. Do not be discouraged when others are not as excited about the vision as you are. Remember, it is your God given vision and many will not understand until the vision is executed. God will send divine connections and those He has divinely ordained to connect with you along the way to accomplish what He has given you to do. Here are a few lessons I learned during my isolation period that helped me in my Kingdom assignment as an entrepreneur. I learned:

1. To make tough business decisions on my own.

During the period of isolation, because I drew closer to God, my discernment sharpened, my ability to tune into the voice of God at a higher level was elevated, and therefore I felt confident with making tough business decisions on my own, I could consult with the Father and hear from Him clearly.

2. To always do my own research.

We have to do our due diligence in everything. Yes, I talk a lot about prayer and hearing from God, but God also wants us to use wisdom and gain the knowledge we need to be the experts in our professions.

3. Not to back down from what I want to see in my business, even when someone tells me no.

In other words, I have learned when there is a will, there is a way. People will tell you no or you cannot do something because they do not want to do it, or they do not know how. Never give up from the first no. Be persistent and go after what you want your business to look like, even if it has not been done before.

4. To never allow the opinions of others to alter the God-given vision of my business.

This one is something I see so often with new entrepreneurs. They will allow someone else to give them an opinion that will completely change the vision God gave them. Stand firm in what God told you to do.

5. To Be BOLD.

Remember who you are and who you belong to. You are a child of the Most High King and God specifically chose you for this. Be bold in knowing you are fulfilling the assignment of the Lord and He will be with you every step of the way.

One thing I had to do as a part of my process was work for someone else.

Before I started my real estate company and before I even got into real estate, I was working for an insurance company, a job I absolutely did not like. Every day I would go to work and say to myself, God, why am I here! I hated going there every day. I did not realize this job was simply one of the places God brought me to equip me for my next destination. This job taught me discipline. If I can work for someone else 8 hours per day, I should be able to work for myself for the same time and then some.

As an entrepreneur, no one is going to tell you what time you have to be at work and what time you can come home. It is all on you. If you do not put in the work, you will not get paid. So, while we have the freedom to create our own schedules, we still have to make sure we are putting in the work required to be successful at our businesses. I also picked up other skills at this job as well. The job was very stressful, and it required me to pay close attention to detail. I learned how to deal with intense situations in the workplace and took this skill with me when it was time for me to run my company.

Another lesson I learned during my processing season was humility. God really taught me some things in this department. I am thankful He did because no matter how much success I have or how much money I make, I will always give Him the Glory and I will always remain humble.

I remember a time when I was working as a real estate agent for a small company and at the time my husband and I were really struggling financially. I remember this particular week I had a real estate closing and my bank account was literally in the red. I knew I could pick up my check from my company on Tuesday, so I literally preserved the gas in my car that week just so I would have enough gas to go pick up my check and go to the bank. Well, Tuesday came, and I went to the office to pick up my check and when I got there the admin said she could not give it to me because our broker had not processed my check. I told her I really needed my check that day. So, she called the broker, and he said, "If she needs it today, she can drive to my house to get it." His house was about 30 more minutes of driving and I literally had to pray my car would make it. God answered my prayers, and I made it. When I got there, he was just relaxing and going on about his day. He had no clue I had to pray my car would make it to his house because I had no gas money, and he had no clue my bank account was negative. He was just living his life with no empathy toward his agent.

From that day forward, I said if I am ever the owner of a business and I have people working for me, I will always pay them what I owe and on time to the best of my ability. I always remember that story when I have to pay my employees now. I learned you never know what someone is going through and what it took for them just to show up. I will forever be grateful to God for that lesson. Was it a fun lesson to go through? Absolutely not, but it was necessary.

Do not allow your process to cause you to quit. Many will quit during the process because they mistakenly label the process as failure, and it is not. The enemy will try to tell you that you are failing, and you need to quit or find something else to do. I came to tell you today the devil is a liar, and the truth is not in him. He sees your future and how bright it is. He is going to do everything in his power to stop it by sending you negative thoughts and trying to convince you that your business idea will not work. Consistency will take you a long way. There is no shortcut to real success. In anything worth having or building, there is always a process. In every process, there must be consistency. Often we get frustrated and impatient because we do not see results right away. The biggest mistake we make is quitting before the harvest comes. Galatians 6:9, "And let us not be weary in well doing: for in due season we shall reap, if we faint not." In other words, if we remain consistent in our endeavors, in due time, we will reap a harvest.

I see so many new business owners make the mistake of not being consistent. Many will quit when they do not see the results fast enough. When a farmer plants his seeds in the ground, he is not expecting to go back tomorrow to harvest the crop. The farmer understands there is a process the seed must go through in order for the crop to grow. The farmer also understands there are certain tasks which must be performed consistently by the farmer to insure the growth of the crop. The farmer must water the crop, keep pests from it and remove any weeds from it that may hinder the growth. The farmer understands if he or she does their part, then the natural process the seed goes through to become a crop will happen. As Entrepreneurs, we must take this approach with our businesses. We cannot expect to collect a harvest during a growth season. We certainly cannot expect to collect a harvest during the planting season. We must remain consistent in well doing, and we must understand the season we are in as an entrepreneur. Are you in the planting season? A season where you may be just starting out and you are planting seeds about your business. If this is the season you are in, then you should be consistent in planting those seeds. This is the task you should be completing consistently during this time.

Have you reached a growth season? The season where those seeds you have planted have started to bloom? They have not reached full maturation, but they are growing. This is a season where you may be stretched as an entrepreneur. This is the time where you may be experiencing something new and learning new things to help grow your business. This is a time where you may be a little uncomfortable having to learn a new skill or overcome some of your fears which are necessary for your personal growth and business growth.

I used to have a fear of public speaking, but I quickly learned I had to get over this fear if I wanted my business to grow. So, even in a growth season, it is important to stay consistent in planting seeds and continuing to grow. The one constant thing I have learned as a Kingdom Entrepreneur, regardless of the season I am in, I must stay consistent with my prayer life and in the Word of God. I really hope this inspires you today to keep going and pushing through your process. Ask God what He is teaching you in this season so you can master the lesson and get promoted to your next level.

Never Lose Sight of
the Vision

When God gives you a vision, He never considers your current situation or circumstances as a prerequisite. What we must realize is the vision He is giving you is not new to Him. It was already done in Heaven. It is your responsibility to manifest it on Earth with God as your guide and helper.

Having a goal or a vision you want to accomplish does not always come easy. The true definition of vision is having the ability to see beyond where you are right now and having the faith to believe you will get there. When one truly has vision, they will push past their fears and insecurities to reach the end goal. The vision is what will keep you going when things get tough. Reading this book and using the interactive journal I have created for the next 21 days will be a defining moment in your life. It will be a time you will remember as a time of faith, action, and perseverance.

Today is the start of seeing your dreams become reality. One of the most important lessons I have learned throughout my journey as an entrepreneur is I must stay focused, build on my gifts, always remain a student, and not be influenced by the opinions of other people. Writing your goals and dreams is very important. Habakkuk 2:2 says, "And the Lord answered me and said write the vision and make it plain upon tables that he may run and readeth it."

In other words, if you write your vision, you can visualize it, process it, and take action. If we can only see the end goal and not what comes in between, it becomes overwhelming and appears to be impossible to accomplish. If we write the end goal and each step in between to get to the end goal, it helps us to tackle one task at a time. It gives us hope as we make small victories that we are on the right path to experiencing the huge WIN. Be sure to refer to Day 1 of the 21 Days of Encouragement journal for your Bible verse, affirmation, and action step.

I also know what it is like to have a big dream or vision, but do not know where and how to start. I know what it feels like to doubt yourself and not think you are smart enough or wise enough to actually do it. Although I was having those doubtful thoughts, the vision I had of starting my own company kept tugging at my heart and would not go away. Many of us have felt inadequate for many reasons. Usually, it is because of our past or where we come from. It is okay to have a past as we all do, but it is not ok to stay stuck in the past. Dwelling on your past is a dream killer. Our past molds us and teaches us. Our past builds our character, so we can handle what the future holds for us.

I was raised with 4 other siblings by a single mother. Money was very tight in our household, but my mom did the best she could. Even as a young child growing up in that environment, I knew I wanted more. I knew even though poverty was around me; it was not my portion, and I did not have to be a product of my environment. We can easily become victims of our environments because it is all we know. The reality is you do not know what you do not know.

As I got older and went away to college, I realized everyone did not grow up like me; some people grew up with their mother and father in the household and everyone did not grow up struggling financially. It opened my eyes to show me there is more to life than what I had seen. All I knew was that I wanted more, and I would work hard to get it. To manifest our dreams, we must have vision beyond what we can only see with our natural eyes. We must be able to see where we are going instead of focusing on where we currently are.

Exposure is also key. What I mean by that is getting exposed to the people and environments of where you want to go in life. I saw and spent time with people who were actually living the life I dreamed of, and they were making it happen. This type of exposure lit a fire in me to work harder. It also encouraged me and helped me to see that if they could do it, then I could too. During my journey, I was connected to some amazing people who helped me to see beyond what I could currently see. My advice to entrepreneurs or anyone who has a dream they are trying to accomplish is to be intentional about meeting and being around people who are in the position of where you are striving to be.

When I started my real estate company, it all began as an idea in my head. Then I picked up a pen and paper and wrote things down. I wrote out the name; I wrote my company's colors and how I wanted my company to operate. Once I could get it all down on paper, I began to visualize it and could actually see how things would fall into place. Once again, writing the vision and making it plain is so simple, but extremely powerful. It is so important for you to make the vision clear. Be specific about what you want and what you want to accomplish. Your specificity is what God needs to hear and see so He can give you exactly what you desire. We are never responsible for the outcome. God is. However, we are responsible for the decisions we make and how we choose to show up daily as it pertains to us manifesting our dreams and visions.

Is there a dream you have or some burning desire you have that just will not seem to go away? Well, if there is, I can promise you it is God who has placed that something there and that feeling will never go away until you have accomplished it. He created all of us for His purpose and for His Glory. We all have a significant contribution we have to make while we are here, and if we do not make that contribution, our lives will feel empty and meaningless. I am here to tell you if you are feeling like you do not know what you should be doing or how you should be doing it, then the first thing to do to get started is to pray. Prayer will change your entire life. Consistent prayer will literally pull down the things God spoke about you in Heaven and have it manifest here on earth. I can speak boldly about this subject because I have experienced it for myself and literally watched the things I prayed for and believed in God to become reality happen right in front of my eyes. Prayer is direct communication with God, and when you do it often and consistently, your life will never be the same.

New levels are reached in our lives, both spiritually and naturally, when we pray. During prayer, we are strengthened. We receive instructions from God and often God will show us ourselves. When I say show us ourselves, I mean He will reveal to you the things you need to work on becoming a better you. He shows us these things because He loves us and He wants us to be the best we can be. He is our Father, and He wants the best for His children. God has revealed myself to me so many times during prayer. I can remember a time when I was praying to God about my husband, asking God to change some things about him, and the Holy Spirit stop me in the middle of my prayer and said, "You need to be praying for God to change some things about you, such as, having patience, such as holding your tongue sometimes, and the list could go on". This is just one example because I could probably write a whole book on the many different revelations about myself God has shown me during prayer.

Having a consistent prayer life will open so many doors for you because you will live a spirit led life. Leading a spirit led life comes with so many benefits. You no longer think and act like those who are in the world, but you think and act as the spirit of God who lives inside of you. I truly believe anyone who does not have a consistent prayer life is literally walking around aimlessly and spiritually blind. The spirit realm is real, and nothing happens in the natural before it happens in the spiritual realm. Our prayers and relationship with our Heavenly Father are what pull those things down from the spiritual realm to the natural.

The Bible tells us:

"Greater is He that is in you, than he that is in the world."

1 John 4:6

This Bible verse tells me I have complete access to greatness, which already lives inside of me. It is up to me to tap into what I already have living inside of me. One of the most important ways to tap into it is to pray.

With all that being said, let us talk about a strategy for our consistent prayer time with God. I have compiled a few suggestions to help:

1. We should try to designate a specific place we have sanctified as our meeting place with God. For me, it is my closet. It could be wherever you like in your home. It should be somewhere quiet and private, where you can spend time with your Heavenly Father.

2. Be intentional about your prayer life by setting a specific time every day you want to meet with God to pray. Your prayer time should be a daily appointment on your calendar with God. Do not allow this time to become a religious ritual, because it should not be. This is genuine time; one you have intentionally set aside to spend with your Father. If we are intentional about nurturing the relationships and spending time with the people we love and care about, why would not we do the same with God?

3. If you choose to, you can also put on some praise and worship music. Praise and worship music shifts the atmosphere. It helps to bring our focus and attention to God as we prepare to go before the throne and enter into His presence.

4. As we go before the Lord in prayer, we want to start out by thanking and praising Him. We want to show Him reverence and honor Him for who He is. God delights in our worship. Praise and worship are the catalyst that change the atmosphere and invite God's presence to surround us. This is my favorite part of worship because His presence is so sweet and amazing. It's like getting drunk in the spirit of God and it feels amazing. When you feel His presence during your worship, you will repent of your sins because when there is true worship, there is also conviction. I will give you an example: As a child, if you know you did something wrong and your parents come into the room and you know they know you did something wrong, you feel convicted to apologize. It is the same with God. We have invited Him into the room with us and we know He knows our wrongdoings, so we repent and ask for forgiveness. When we go before the Father in prayer, we want to be free and clean of sin. Sin separates us from God, but because the blood of Jesus has redeemed us, we simply have to ask for forgiveness, and He will forgive.

5. Now that we have given Him praise and worship and have asked for repentance, we can now freely talk to our heavenly Father. We can freely make our requests known and ask for guidance in every area of our lives. When we pray, we should come to our Father in confidence, knowing He hears our prayers. Ephesians 3:12 says, "We have boldness and confident access through faith in him." We have been granted direct access to God through Jesus Christ. Matthew 21:22 says, "And all things whatsoever ye shall ask in prayer, believing, ye shall receive." During this time, talk to God and commune with Him and ask Him whatever you want. Ask Him to guide you to live a spirit led life.

6. Finally, take a moment to be still and quiet. Take this time to simply listen and allow Him to speak back to you. Many times, in these moments, I receive answers, instructions and revelations. I would also encourage you to keep a journal with you to write what you hear from God. You will also want to have your Bible as well. During this time, it is imperative to read and study God's Word; reading a passage of scripture before or after prayer however you are led by the Holy Spirit. The Word of God is your guidance. The Word of God is confirmation of what you are hearing from God during your prayer time. If what you are hearing is in alignment with God's Word, then that is your confirmation.

This is a prayer you can say every day until God reveals answers:

"Dear God, Thank You for creating me in Your image and giving me a special purpose. I thank You for Your spirit living in me and because of that I can do All Things through You, who gives me strength. I thank You for placing purpose and vision in my life. I will listen and obey You even when it's uncomfortable for me. I thank You for my spiritual ears being open and You being the guiding force in my life. I thank You for giving me specific instructions on what it is You are calling me to do. I love You, I trust You, and I will obey You in Jesus' name I pray. Amen."

The word of God tells us that God knew us before we were born. Jeremiah 1:4-5 (NLT) says, "I knew you before I formed you in your mother's womb. Before you were born, I set you apart and appointed you as my prophet to the nations." This was God himself telling Jeremiah He knew him before he was born, and He already predestined his future and what he was called to do. Well,

God did this same exact thing for you and me. He knew us before we hit our mother's womb and He already knew what He wanted us to do once we got there. With that being said, please know the vision you have of the things you want to accomplish came straight from God.

I remember a time when I almost lost sight of the vision. I almost completely quit real estate because of a deal that went really wrong, and I had to get an attorney involved to represent myself and my client. As a new agent, I did not use the proper language in a contract which could have resulted in a lawsuit. Thank goodness no lawsuits were filed. This deal had me so stressed out I was losing sleep at night. I was so frustrated with this deal, I just wanted to quit real estate altogether. After the situation was resolved, I left the industry for a year. I am so thankful I came back. The vision God gave me kept pulling me in, and I knew something did not feel right when I left.

I cannot believe that I almost quit the thing that started my entrepreneurship journey and allowed me to birth other businesses through my real estate career. At the time, I did not realize I was in my processing season, and God was simply teaching me what I should do if this situation ever occurred again. Little did I know, He had me go through this situation because He knew one day I would have my own real estate company and one of my agents would actually come to me with this same situation. I was able to advise them on what to do so they would not experience what I did. I almost lost sight of the vision because I did not realize during the situation, God was simply giving me the wisdom and knowledge I needed to lead others in my field.

I have learned countless lessons during my entrepreneurship journey that I could have mistaken for failures when, in actuality, they were lessons. They were lessons that gave me the wisdom and knowledge I needed to manifest the vision. What I hope this book will teach Kingdom Entrepreneurs is that the manifestation of the vision makes it all worth it. The price we pay to get to where God is taking us is the cost of our entrepreneur anointing. You were anointed to be an entrepreneur. It was not something you just decided to do or try out. God specifically chose you for this. Whenever you see an entrepreneur who is thriving and doing well in what they have been called to do, just know there was a price he or she had to pay to get there.

As an entrepreneur, you should never be afraid to charge someone for your knowledge or services. You paid a price to get the knowledge you have, and anyone seeking that knowledge should rightfully pay you for sharing it.

Distractions can also cause you to lose sight of the vision. This is one of the biggest hindrance I see with people who have a God-given vision. The enemy will send distractions to knock you off your post. The enemy knows if your God-given vision is manifested, it will be a threat to the enemy and all of his tactics. The enemy does not want to see Kingdom Entrepreneurs succeed because he knows God placed them in position so they can fund Kingdom Projects. He will try to send distractions through people, through other projects God has not called you to, and even through our daily routines. You know you are dealing with a distraction if it is taking you in the opposite direction of the vision God gave you.

Sometimes the people we allow in our space can be a distraction because they do not understand the vision God gave you and they are not interested in seeing you accomplish it. Allowing the wrong people to have access to you is an open door to heeding to other voices not meant for you to listen to in this season of your life. I do not think we realize how much of an influence others can have on us when we allow them to speak into our lives on a consistent basis. It is inevitable you will start to talk and act like the people you are consistently around. So here is what I gather from this statement. If I know the influence of others could potentially be a distraction from reaching my destiny, I need to first make sure I am confident in knowing who I am. My confidence and knowing who I am will come from me spending time with God. If I truly know Him, I will be able to discern the relationships in my life which are divinely ordained, and the ones sent by the enemy as a distraction.

Stay focused on the vision and ask God to help you discern distractions. Be mindful, everything you have set out to do is possible with God in the forefront of your life.

How many times have we thought about something or hoped for something and shied away from it because we are so focused on what it will take to get to the end result? The end result of what we hope for is the measure of our faith. Hebrews 11:1, "Faith is the substance of things hoped for and the evidence of things not seen." To believe the thing you hope for is already done is called faith activation. Your faith can take you far, but without the work behind it, the end result will never be manifested.

As stated in my 21 Days of Encouragement journal for Day Six, the Bible verse for today is James 2:20 (KJV), "But wilt thou know, O vain man that faith without works is dead." God will give you a vision, sometimes big and sometimes small, but in order for it to manifest, there must be work involved. I often think of the story of Noah in the bible. God commissioned Noah to build an ark big enough for his entire family and for 2 of each kind of animal. Can you imagine the long hours and work involved to get that done? The biggest takeaway from this story is Noah had the faith to believe what God said was going to happen. He believed the flood was coming because God said so. He did not try to rationalize or think with human logic that this might not happen because it had not rained there in so long. He simply took God's promise for what it was and then acted on it. Noah believed what God said, and that was the faith part. Noah started to put the required action needed behind the faith by starting the construction of the Ark. He had to take the first step to start and build the ark and as he began to build, God gave him further instructions.

What has God promised you? Do you believe the promise? If so, have you started to build on that promise? What action steps do you need to take to put behind your faith? Will you allow what you see right now to hinder you from working toward your final goal?

I want to share with you the process I went through while writing this book. I am going to be very transparent about this. I believe this will help you see there is a process in anything we want to accomplish. I wish I could shorten the process for you, but unfortunately, I cannot. First, I will start by saying writing a book had never been a dream of mine, however it was a vision God placed in my heart to do a few years ago. He instructed me to write a whole book. I am laughing to myself now because when I was given the vision, I never thought I could do it. I never thought I would have the self-discipline or time to pull this off. I even asked God why He would want me to write this book and I kept hearing, "I want them to hear your story". Telling my story requires complete transparency and possibly me sharing things with people I do not want them to know. So, I began writing the book, not really knowing what I wanted to write and how much I should share. I have pages of material in so many journals and on my phone where I started writing and did not finish or decided to start over. There would be times I would write every day consistently and then put it down for a while. The road ahead to get the book completed seemed so far away. It seemed like I was fighting an uphill battle that never ended. I could not understand why it was so difficult for me. I had to realize too, the story was being created day by day and God's timing is perfect. He was slowly, but surely, writing my story, and it would have to be released at the right time.

Later, I met a well-known author at a networking event and I shared with him what I was dealing with in trying to write this book. He said something so simple but so profound, and it helped me to put everything into perspective. He said, write one paragraph per day. He said that if you break it up into small pieces, it will not seem like the goal is impossible to reach. I believe this advice can apply to anything you are trying to accomplish in life. The best analogy I can think of to describe this is that you cannot swallow a steak whole. If you try, you will choke. However, you can cut it into pieces and eat, one piece at a time. I learned I was trying to eat my steak whole when I was writing my book. I was trying to finish it all too quickly instead of allowing myself to take it one day at a time. I was only focusing on the end result and not focusing on and accepting the process it would take for me to get the book done. Once you accept the process and not just the result, you will do the work. When there is a vision, there will be a process. The end result of your vision will manifest when you believe it can be done and you put the work into making it happen.

The big question to ask all the Kingdom Entrepreneurs is: How will you respond when your faith is being tested?

Faith is the thing we have that says we believe what we hope for is already done. Faith says no matter what my current situation looks like... I STILL BELIEVE. Some have bigger faith than others and I would be remiss to say our faith is never tested. My faith has been tested countless times on this journey we call life. It's been tested in my marriage, with my children, my health, and most definitely in my business. I could tell you about many stories of how I had nothing else to stand on but my faith. There were times where I had nowhere to turn but to God because my back was completely up against a wall. One thing I know for sure is God is real, and my faith will never waiver because I have seen Him firsthand in my life. It is necessary for your faith to be tested for your faith to grow.

During the times of your faith being tested, there are certain things which happen in this process:

1. You recognize God is in control
2. Your Character is being refined
3. Your Faith increases

This reminds me of a time when I had nothing but my faith to stand on. In the Book of Genesis, Chapter 12, God told Abram to leave his native country, his relatives, and his father's family. God told him to go to a land He would show him. God never gave him the exact location of where he was going or even how he would get there. God just simply said, "GO!!"

When I read this passage of scripture, I am reminded of my journey as an entrepreneur. I knew God wanted me to travel down this path of entrepreneurship, but He never showed me how I would get there and what I would have to go through during the journey. He just simply said, "Go forth and BE!" Many times, during this journey, my faith was tested. Although I knew the vision, He showed me, my current circumstances did not line up with the vision. The vision is what keeps you going, and faith is what brings you to the vision.

Most of the time, the area in your life where God has called you to is the area we often struggle with. God called me to be wealthy and to help break generational curses of poverty. I knew this was what He called me to do, but yet I kept struggling with my finances.

Is there an area in your life you continue to struggle with? If it is, take note of that area and pay attention to the lessons God is trying to teach you during your struggle season. None of what we go through is in vain. I truly believe the areas we struggle in will be the areas we not only thrive in, but can also bring others out of those same struggles.

Back in 2011, when God told me to leave Corporate America and pursue real estate full-time, it took crazy faith to be willing to give up what I felt was secure to pursue something I knew nothing about. One thing I have learned with my walk with God is when He says move You have got to MOVE! Little did I know the leap of faith I took back then is what brought me to where I am today.

As I have gone through the journey day after day, my faith has gotten stronger. As we continue to trust Him and walk by faith, He will continue to take us from faith to faith and glory to glory. What I have learned during this journey is taking the perceived easier road can lead to death of the vision. I could have decided to do what was easy and familiar to me instead of heeding to the voice of God and stepping out on faith. If I would have taken the easier route, I probably would not be here, or my path may have taken much longer than God intended it to.

We can prolong our destiny when it does not have to be prolonged. Disobedience and lack of faith are two of the biggest hindrances in causing us to become stuck and stagnant. God wants us to totally submit to Him and trust Him. The Bible tells us in Psalm 37:23, "The steps of a good man are ordered by God." In this passage of scripture, it uses the word good to describe the type of person whose steps are ordered by God. The definition of "good" is to be desired or approved of. It also means morally right; righteousness. Who are the good men they are referring to in this passage of scripture? The good men are those who are believers and who have been deemed righteous through Christ Jesus. With that being said, we have already met the first requirement of being good, and now we just have to submit to Him when He orders our steps. I know I make it sound so easy to do. It is not always easy, but the instruction of obeying is simple. Obedience will always yield the manifestation of the vision.

You Have Been Called to Stand Out

The fact that not one person on this earth has the same DNA is a good indication God never intended for us to fit in or to try to be like someone else. Often, as we are growing up, we feel the need to fit in with others because we have not truly discovered who we are yet. Unfortunately, there are full-grown adults who still feel the need to fit in. I would have to say it is for the same reason they are still unaware of who they are.

As entrepreneurs, we are called to bring forth something new. When I say new, it does not always mean a product or service no one has ever sold before, however it is a product or service YOU will be selling for the first time in your own unique way. No one can do what I do, the way I do it, because I am the only Me in this world. No one can do what you do, the way you do it, because you are the only YOU in this world. This is something God wants us to take pride in and not be ashamed of because He specifically took the time to create you uniquely different from every individual in the world. It gives Him joy to see your uniqueness shining to give Him Glory. I want you to remember this every time you feel a need to try to fit in with people who God never intended you to be like.

Give your uniqueness a voice. Discover the thing that makes you different, embrace it and shout it from the rooftops. Use that uniqueness in your business, in your relationships, and in every area of your life. This uniqueness is what will attract the right customers for your business, the right people for your organization, and for your business relationships.

Thinking back to my childhood and teenage years, I have always been soft-spoken and not one who talks a lot. All my siblings and I are far apart in age. My two older brothers are 7 and 4 years older than I am. My younger brother is 8 years younger than me, and my sister is 15 years younger. I was right in the middle. Because I did not really have siblings my age and for a long time, I was the only girl; I spent a lot of time playing alone in my room as a kid. I played with my dolls; I played dress up; I used to pretend I was a teacher, and my dolls would be the class. I was never the type of person who needed to have people around me to have fun. I enjoyed my own company and still do now. I truly believe often as entrepreneurs you have to be ok with being alone. You must be ok with deciding alone and being the first to make moves sometimes. You have to be ok knowing you will not always have cheerleaders cheering you on. As a matter of fact, you may have no one cheering you on. It's not always because they do not want to see you succeed, but more often than not, it is because they do not understand your vision. As an entrepreneur, you have to be ok with people not understanding. You cannot harbor any bitter feelings toward them because the vision was given to you. God only gave you the ability to see something before it was actually manifested. I think it is an honor and a privilege; God specifically chose you to bring forth a vision only you can see. So, let's change our perspective when people do not get the vision, or they do not support the vision. Instead of being angry or hurt towards them, lift your hands, and say, "Thank You, God, for choosing me to execute Your vision." Ephesians 2:10 says, "For we are His workmanship created in Christ Jesus for good works, which God prepared beforehand, that we should walk in them."

We were each made specifically to stand out because our Father in Heaven took the time to create us. He took the time to give each of us specific and unique qualities and gifts for us to use while we are here on Earth and to walk in them boldly. Today, I challenge you to find your uniqueness and run with it. The thing that is unique about you is the thing that will help others. Suppressing your uniqueness only delays your destiny.

It is human nature for us to want to give up or quit when things are not going well. As entrepreneurs, you will go through storms. It is inevitable. Did you know God wants to use your storms, too? He will use everything you have gone through to mold you into the person He intended for you to be. Your journey is simply that... YOURS. Never compare your journey to someone else's because God has specifically designed your journey just for you. He knows why we have to go through what we are going through, because God sees where He is taking us and how we will get there. I want you to rest in knowing God knows exactly what He is doing. He will never steer you wrong. Often, the storms we go through are a stepping-stone to our next level. Our storms can also be a huge part of our uniqueness, so do not be ashamed of what you have gone through. Allow God to use your unique storms to push you to your place of overflow. The overflow is where you are not only healed and thriving but also being used by God through your testimony and your uniqueness to heal others.

How many times have I heard people say, 'What is my purpose?' It's been too many to count. As believers, we all have the same purpose, which is to Give God Glory and to build His Kingdom. It is just that simple. However, God gives all of us different ways to do it. So, in order for you to discover the vehicle He wants to give you to fulfill your purpose, then you must seek Him above all things, and He will show you what that vehicle is. The Bible tells us in Matthew 6:33," To seek the Kingdom of God above all else and live righteously and He will give you everything you need." So, when we focus on Him, we will gain clarity, focus and direction on the who, what, when, where, and why.

The vehicle God released to me to help with fulfilling my purpose is real estate. Real Estate is merely my profession and NOT my purpose. Through this profession, I can touch the lives of many, help build God's Kingdom, educate and assist people with becoming homeowners, investors, and learn about other aspects of real estate.

When I really figured out my purpose, or my part in glorifying God and building His Kingdom, I was already working in the real estate field. I received a revelation from God one day as I was doing my regular duties as a real estate agent. I will never forget this day because it was a defining moment in my life. It was a warm spring day, and I was about 32 years old. I started my real estate career about 2 years prior to this and I was still trying to find my way in the business. On this particular day, I received a referral from my husband for one of his mortgage clients. He told me she needed to sell her home and asked me to contact her so we could meet. I had never met this woman and did not know who she was. We spoke, and she asked me to come to her home that same day so I could see the house she wanted to sell. I was excited and pumped because I was anticipating getting a new listing. As I pulled up to the home, I was a little disappointed because of the condition of the home. I knew to get it sold quickly, some work would need to be done on the property. As I proceed to get out of the car and walk up to the door, I was taking mental notes of things I saw outside that could use a little work. I rang the doorbell and a middle-aged Caucasian woman came to the door. She was about two or three inches taller than me, with curly brown hair, and was barefoot. I remember walking in the house and I just felt a somber spirit come over me. The inside of the home needed just as much work as the outside, if not more. I asked her to give me a tour of the property and she did. Then we sat down at her kitchen table to talk. I remember we had not even talked about the house yet and she began to talk to me about everything going on in her life and how overwhelmed she was. She told me her mother was very sick, and she could not take care of herself anymore. She told me she was going back and forth from her house to her mother's house to take care of her while still working a full-time job. Then she started to cry. I have to admit, at first, I was a bit uncomfortable; I did not know what to say or what to do. This was the first time I had been in a situation like this with a complete stranger.

As I was sitting there, I heard a small, still voice in my ear say, "You need to pray with her." I was nervous and felt awkward, so I tried to ignore the voice, but it would not go away. I heard the voice again and this time I heard, "You better not leave this house without praying for this woman." Looking back at that moment, it makes me chuckle a little at how the Holy Spirit gave me that last warning. The Holy Spirit is our teacher and sometimes has to deal with us just like normal teachers would. I felt the Holy Spirit had to deal with me in that way and I am so glad I obeyed. I had no clue how important my obedience was at that moment in my life and in the woman's life I prayed for.

I politely asked her if she minded if I prayed with her. She said, "I would love that." So, I grabbed her hands, and we prayed. Tears fell, and we truly felt the power of God's presence in her home that day. Before I left, she thanked me and said she really felt better. She said she felt like a weight had been lifted off her shoulders. What I realized is by praying with her, it shifted her focus off of her problems and shifted her focus on GOD. That is what He wants us to do so we can fulfill our purpose.

When I got in my car to go home, I felt like a light bulb came on. I felt like I discovered something amazing. I was so excited I had helped someone shift their focus back to God and helped to pull someone I did not even know out of a dark place and simply showed her the light. The light was God, and I was just a vessel used to take her to Him. I was so excited and happy and I did not even get the listing because, after discussing everything that was going on, she decided not to sell. Despite all of that, I was on cloud nine because God revealed my purpose in that meeting. That day He showed me I am not just a real estate agent who sells houses, but I am an ambassador for Christ and my purpose is to bring Him Glory, build His Kingdom by directing people back to Him through prayer. He showed me He would use real estate as my way of reaching God's people, and if I focused on the purpose and NOT the sale; He assured me the sales would come. When you chase purpose and not money, you will always win.

When God Sends You You cannot fail!

As a Kingdom Entrepreneur, you have been given an assignment. You have been tasked to be creative, innovative and, in most cases, to be a pioneer in your industry or whatever area of business God has called you to. Sometimes you have to be the first one to do something. Sometimes you must be the first one to make a move. Did you know when you are given a Kingdom assignment, the destiny of others God has assigned to you depends on you being the first? God did not make any mistakes when He chose you for the assignment. He equipped you at birth with all that you need, and the rest is developed during your process. The plan has already been mapped out. You just have to walk it out and see it through.

I believe one way for Kingdom entrepreneurs to overcome the feeling of failure is to first understand you are not alone. You must realize when God sends you, you cannot fail. I am reminded of the story of Gideon found in Judges chapters 6-8. God sent him to lead an army of men in battle and they were victorious. In the story, it talks about how Gideon was considered to be the least of his people, but God chose him anyway. Not only did God choose the one the world considered weak, but He also instructed him to only take a small number of soldiers with him to battle. This is the type of story that demonstrates how God will set you up to win without using what society thinks success should look like or how it should be achieved. God will always put you in a position where He gets the Glory. Frankly, this is the best position to be in because you are the beneficiary of the reward. He allowed Gideon and his army to experience the victory, but God gets the Glory.

Just like God orchestrated this moment for him, He is doing the same for you in your life and in your business. I just want to bring your attention to Judges 6:14, "Then the Lord turned to him and said, ' Go with the strength you have, and rescue Israel from the Midianites. I am sending you!'" Can we just focus on that verse for a minute? God is telling Gideon to go with the strength that he has, and he reminds him he is being sent by God! This is so powerful on so many levels. First, it lets us know all we can do is go with the strength we have and depend on God for the rest. Secondly, it reminds us God Himself sent us. So, if God Himself sent you, then you cannot fail. The reason I love this story so much is because the outcome of the battle is not based on Gideon's abilities, it is all on God. When you have been sent on assignment by God, the outcome is out of your hands. You will go with the strength you have, but God will go with you if you let Him. His strength is undeniable and with Him, you will win.

From as far back as I can remember, I have always been an entrepreneur. Even as a child, before I could even spell the word or knew what it was, I always had some type of business. Looking back, it is just confirmation this is what God has called me to. If you are an entrepreneur or aspire to be one, you can probably relate to what I am saying. Here are a few clues you may have been called to entrepreneurship:

1. You are always coming up with ideas to make money.

2. You can take what someone may be doing for a hobby, or just pleasure, and show them how they can turn it into a business.

3. You were probably always unhappy in a 9-5 setting because you felt as though you could be doing more.

4. As a kid, or even as an adult, you always had a side business.

I remember as a little girl when I was in the third grade, I made fake nails from glue and would sell them to the little girls in my class. I also remember having a flower business. I would pick flowers from the neighbors' yards and go door to door selling them. It's funny when I think about it because back then, at such a young age, I always had some type of hustle going on. My mom always tells the story of when I was in second grade, she bought my school pictures. When my teacher sent the pictures home with me, instead of me giving them to my mom right away, once again I went around the neighborhood selling them. My mom found out because one neighbor came to my mom and brought the picture back to her and said she did not think my mom knew I was selling my school pictures to people. Of course, she did not know, but she thought it was funny. To this day, she always tells people this story about me when they talk about me being an entrepreneur. Being an entrepreneur has always been a part of me. It was something that came naturally to me even before I knew there was a word for what I was passionate about doing.

As we were growing up, it was always instilled in us to go to college so we could get a good job. There is nothing wrong with advocating for higher education because I fully support it, but going to college does not automatically guarantee you will get a good job. To be honest, how is a good job defined, anyway? Is it having benefits, or making a six-figure salary? What is a good job? I have always believed if someone can put a cap on how much money you can make, it is not a good job. Do not get me wrong, I am not knocking those with 9-5 jobs, but what I am saying is if you have one, you do not have to limit yourself there.

I started out working a 9-5 job after graduating college. I worked there for 7 years, and the most I ever made was $44,000 per year. Back then I thought that was a decent amount of money, but now as an entrepreneur I can say the amount of money I made working for one year, I have made in a month or even a week. There is no cap on your income as an entrepreneur. Being an entrepreneur provides you with limitless opportunities, depending on how hard you work and your consistency.

My journey began in 2005 when I first got my real estate license. I was excited, young, and ready to take on the world. During that time, the real estate market was booming, so everyone in real estate was doing well. I left my job and was determined to sell real estate full-time. I did pretty well the first two years, but once 2008 hit, the real estate market crashed. My sales back then were few and far between. Because of the market at the time and me not knowing how to sustain my real estate business in this type of market, I had to go back to work. Our family began to suffer financially, and one income was not enough to sustain us. I truly felt God was sending me back to learn discipline. One thing about being an entrepreneur, an alarm clock should not have to wake you up, but your end goal and your vision for yourself and your family should. Before I left my job the first time, my vision was not clear and therefore I was not able to be disciplined enough to follow through and be successful. How can you travel to a certain destination when you don't know where you are going? If you do not have a clear vision of where you are going, you will be lost and simply going in circles.

When I went back to my job, and thank God, they took me back, I started to realize if I could work for this company from 8am-5pm, then why could I not do the same for my own business? The answer was simple: I had no discipline. God had me work there for 3 more years, and while I was there, I picked up some additional skills my eyes were not open to before. This time, as I worked there, I was not just working to be an employee, but I was actually studying the structure of the company to help me start my own.

One of the biggest lessons I learned from this Fortune 500 company was all the employees were trained to follow a certain process every day. We all knew exactly what we were supposed to do each day when we came in. As an entrepreneur, knowing what to do each day and doing it consistently will produce results. The other thing I picked up was everyone was on a schedule. We all knew what time we had to be at work, had a certain time allotted for lunch and breaks, along with what time we could leave. We all knew what we should be doing in the mornings, and we knew what we should be doing in the afternoons.

Having a schedule is also key to running a business. As an entrepreneur, if you have a schedule, you are able to get things done and maintain your life/work balance. It also eliminates wasted time. Our time is so valuable. Wasted time can never be regained. It is so imperative that we are selective with our time and who we give it to. I learned you have to treat your business as if it were already a Fortune 500 company. When the time comes to scale and grow your business, you will then duplicate the processes you have created through other people, or even through automated systems. Processes and systems are an essential key to growth in your business. So, what does your daily routine look like? I know we may not have the same exact schedule every day, but when you are an entrepreneur, there should be some things on your schedule daily that are consistent for you.

Here is an example of the consistent things I do on my schedule every single day:

5:00 am: Pray and read the bible

6:00am: Facilitate a prayer call

7:00 am: Listen to uplifting videos/podcasts/for personal development

8:00am: Check my schedule for the day, get dressed

9:00 am: Return phone calls and emails

10:00am: Appointments/phone calls/ Income-producing activities.

Just in case you do not understand what an income producing activity is, it simply means to do things in your business that will bring you income. It does not have to be right now income. It could be a phone call or an email that may bring you income months later. But all in all, if it brings you income at some point, it is considered an income producing activity. One thing about being an entrepreneur is, often we have to work overtime before we see the fruits of our labor. For this reason, many fail in business because they are not willing to continue to work, even if they do not see results right away. When you make a commitment to your business to work hard, even when you do not see the results immediately, you are planting seeds for your business. Anytime a seed is planted and watered properly, it is bound to grow. It is the same concept for our businesses.

Now, this is not my schedule every single day, but this is it in a nutshell unless I have something special going on. Once I decided to do these things every day and in this order, my days became more productive and my vision of what I wanted to accomplish became much clearer.

During my time back at my job, I was still determined not to give up on being a real estate agent. I worked my job from 8 to 5 and worked my business after work and on the weekends. I marketed my real estate business to everyone I knew and to strangers, too. On Saturday afternoons, my kids and I would pass out flyers at the mall and pass them out in different neighborhoods I wanted to serve as an agent. They thought it was something fun to do. They were excited to help Mommy with her business. I worked my full-time job and sold real estate for 3 years. I made a lot of sacrifices during this time, but I knew it was temporary and eventually I would be able to be a full-time real estate agent.

Around 2011, after working full- time and as an agent part -time, God spoke and said it was time to leave my job. I was afraid because I remembered what had happened before when I left. While I was working, I saved some money to make sure we would be ok. Even though I was afraid to step out again, I did not let fear stop me. I knew God was speaking, and I had to make my move now. I remember sitting at my desk at work and I was talking to a coworker about my decision to leave the job and become a full-time agent. I remember the tears just flowed because I was afraid, but I knew I had to do it. I also remember when I told others I was leaving my job, people were saying things like: 'Why would you do that?' 'How are you going to get clients?' 'The real estate market is not even good right now?' Yes, this is what I heard from people when God was telling me to do just the opposite. This is where the Kingdom Entrepreneur thing really becomes real. I had to decide to obey God. I had no other choice but to trust Him in my obedience. God does not tell us to do things because it is easy... He tells us to do things because of purpose and so He gets the Glory. He had me leave my job when the real estate market was not good, but He said, "NOW." I am so glad I obeyed the voice of God, instead of listening to the opinions of other people. Looking back at the timing of everything, now I can understand why the timing had to be when it was. Although I could not see all He had in store for me, He certainly knew what was coming down the pipeline.

Many times, when you decide to do something different, people will always try to deter you from it. I believe it is the enemy's way of hindering your destiny. No hard feelings against those who did not understand the vision, they were just unaware and could not see what God wanted to do in my life. Really, why should they understand? This is what God showed me and not them. This is why, as entrepreneurs, we should not get angry with people who do not support our vision because they just do not understand it. My advice is to continue to work hard and manifest the vision so they can see it.

As an entrepreneur, you cannot be afraid to stand out and realize you will be in a position many times where you will be the first to do something. I want to end this chapter with this Bible verse, and I encourage you to add this one to your daily prayers/affirmations. 2 Timothy 1:7, "For God Hath not given us a spirit of fear; but of power, and of love, and of a sound mind." As a Kingdom Entrepreneur, you will be faced with many challenges, but this Bible verse reminds us that we do not have to be afraid; we operate our lives and in the marketplace with love and a sound mind.

Remember, if you are ever feeling afraid, know that fear does not come from God. When this emotion rises in you, combat that emotion with 2 Timothy 1:7, "And decree and declare that word over you and your business. Be confident in knowing you have been sent by God and because of that, you will not fail."

GOD WANTS TO USE YOU

Hey Kingdom Entrepreneur! I know you did not think your business was just business. I know you did not think your main goal was to make money. I hope you understand it is bigger than that. I want you to focus on making sure any and everyone who comes in contact with your business will experience a Kingdom touch. Even if they do not buy anything from you, they will feel the presence of God in your presence or in the presence of your business. The only way Kingdom Entrepreneurs can ensure this type of residue being present in their businesses is by them constantly staying in the presence of God. We must consult with God about everything when it comes to our businesses. We should consult with Him from the concept of the business down to all the minor details of our business. God uses everything we do and everything we accomplish to represent and draw souls to the Kingdom. You are an ambassador for Christ and ultimately, represent His Glory on earth. I do not know about you, but I am honored to be one of His representatives. Since I am His ambassador, I must consult with Him daily. He is my boss and I get all my directions straight from Him.

If you do not remember anything else I have written in this book, I want you to remember this: God created you for three reasons. When you understand these reasons, then you open yourself up to be used in mighty ways by God.

1. He created you to have a relationship with Him. God wants to be your friend. He wants to be your Father, your provider, your peace, your joy, your healer, and everything else you need. If He wants to be all these things to you, then He clearly wants a relationship with you.

2. He wants us to recognize the light we have within us and share that light with others. When we allow our light to shine, it helps others to recognize the light they have within as well, and it becomes a domino effect. When people see you going after your God given vision and are witnessing your results, it inspires them to do the same. These are questions I ask myself daily: Who did I inspire today and who did I help today? Helping and inspiring are Kingdom Requirements for entrepreneurs. If you are not doing these things, how can God trust you to lead? Sometimes we get so focused on making money we forget what truly matters to God. If we stay in a posture of making sure we are concerned about what God is concerned about, the money will come.

3. Our lives are used for His Glory. Everything we do and accomplish as entrepreneurs should point right back to God to give Him the Glory. We are the examples and the ambassadors for Christ.

We are the ones who are here to show others they can experience Heaven on Earth. Our obedience and willingness to surrender to God in our businesses and every aspect of our lives will yield supernatural results.

When you operate with Kingdom Principles, the favor of God will always rest upon you. Do not get caught up in conforming to the world's ideology of what the business world should look like. Always operate in Love, Humility, Honesty, and Faith. These are the core characteristics of a Kingdom Entrepreneur.

As a Kingdom Entrepreneur, we can never forget where our help comes from. We should never idolize entrepreneurship or the things we have accomplished. Idolatry is one of those sins that can separate us from the Will of God. Being outside of God's Will is a dangerous place to be. Jonah 2:8 says, "Those who pay regard to vain idols forsake their hope of steadfast love." We have read about people in the Bible who have created false gods and idols to worship. They actually made them with silver and gold with their own hands. While this is not something we as believers would do in this day and time, we can still be guilty of creating modern- day idols. What do I mean by modern- day idols? A modern-day idol would be anyone or anything you value more than God or prioritize and put before God.

Some of the most common modern-day idols are money, business, and relationships. Yes, these can become our idols when we put them before God. We can get easily caught up in the rat race of chasing a dollar instead of chasing God. This always brings me back to my foundation scripture, which is Matthew 6:33, "Seek Ye first the kingdom of God and all of His righteousness and all of these things will be added unto you." As I am prioritizing my life, the first thing on my list should be a relationship with God. When your relationship with God is good, you will have the grace and strength to handle everything else. If you feel you may be in jeopardy of idolizing someone or something and putting it before God, then ask yourself these few questions:

1. Am I chasing after money, or a relationship more than I am chasing after God?

2. Am I more focused on seeking the validation and approval of others more than I am seeking to please God?

3. Am I building my business only for the money without real purpose behind it?

4. Do I put the building of my business above spending time with God and hearing from Him?

These can be modern- day ways of how we get caught up in idolatry. Psalm 135:15-18 says, "The idols of the nations are silver and gold, the work of human hands. They have mouths, but do not speak, they have eyes, but do not see; they have ears, but do not hear, nor is there any breath in their mouths. Those who make them become like them and so do all who trust in them."

This Bible verse is letting us know idols made by humans are powerless. The idols they created back then had no power and the ones we create in our lives now have no power either. Why on earth would we worship people or things, instead of worshiping the Creator of ALL things? There is nothing wrong with working hard to make your vision come to fruition, but we cannot let it consume us to a point where it is the most important thing in our lives. God must always come first.

The people you decide to partner with in business should also have the same Kingdom Business characteristics. The people you decide to connect with in business can become a hindrance to where God is taking you if they are not also operating with these core characteristics. Your connections do matter. Be mindful about the people you invite to build with. Pray for discernment and simply ask God, "Am I supposed to be in partnership with this person?" God will let you know.

There was someone I was going to partner with in one of my businesses. When we first met, I felt like we hit it off and she seemed to be very knowledgeable. I was getting contracts drawn up to solidify the partnership and every time I would get ready to have the contracts signed, something would come up. I prayed and asked God to show me this person's true character. Before I signed a contract with them, I needed to know. God did just that. He showed me who they really were. Although I was getting small red flags about this person, I still tried to give them another chance.

These were some of the red flags I noticed, and it caused me to ask for clarity from God:

1. There was always confusion and chaos with this person. Sometimes people operate with a spirit of confusion. Know this is not of God because God is a God of order. This person would always have an issue come up on the day of an important meeting or if we had a photo shoot planned for branding. There was always some type of chaos going on in their life. I am not saying people do not go through things because they do, but what I am saying is, it may not be that person's season to be connected with you. You do not want to invite unnecessary spiritual warfare into your life or your business.

2. This person always had excuses about why something was not done. The excuses just did not make sense. They basically had a lying spirit. You can never be in a business relationship with someone who lies because you will not ever be able to trust them. Mistrust in a partnership is detrimental to the business.

3. This person never did what they said they were going to do. They did not honor their word. This is a character flaw, and if you are building a business, you cannot have this type of energy around your business. Being a man or woman of honor is major when it comes to being a Kingdom Entrepreneur. It's important that you connect with people whose words line up with their actions.

I know when we were younger our parents would tell us to watch the company we keep because they understood how detrimental it could be if we were hanging out with the wrong people. They understood that actually allowing the wrong people to speak into our spirit daily and often could change the way we think and ultimately affect the way we act. Yes, it is that serious and although we feel as adults, we are old enough not to succumb to the influence of others, we still do. Whatever you consistently hear and accept in your spirit becomes a part of you. Eventually, you will believe what you hear and begin to act on it.

Who is speaking into your life, and what are they saying? Do the people you spend your time with affirm your destiny or do they speak against it? Pray and ask God to send you divine connections. He will do just that. He will send people who will speak life into you and people who will divinely assist you in reaching your next level.

Not only do we have to watch the words we allow to be spoken in our spirits and over us, but most importantly, we have to watch the words that come out of our mouths. The words that come out of your mouth consistently will literally determine how far you will go. As we know, God created the Heavens and the earth by speaking a word and those things He spoke manifested. We have been given the same power to manifest our dreams with the words we speak. When we say something over and over again, we begin to believe it. When we begin to believe it, we will then act on what we say. Proverbs 18:21 says, "Death and life are in the power of the tongue: and they that love it shall eat the fruit thereof." In other words, the way you choose your words to speak can either fuel your dreams or kill them. Whatever direction you decide will be your portion. It is important that we release into the atmosphere with our words what we want to see happen according to God's Will for our lives. Once you begin to speak it, you are then coming into agreement with the vision God gave you. As you come into agreement with the vision, your actions will line up with the vision as well. I used to use the phrases " I hope it will happen", "If it happens" and "Maybe it will". I have learned to take these words out of my vocabulary and have learned to speak as though it has already happened. Actually, what you are dreaming about has already happened in Heaven, but when we speak it... we are pulling it down from Heaven to manifest on earth. The plan for you was already mapped out by God. You just need to get into agreement with the plan.

Let your words be the oxygen to the manifestation of your vision. Let your words become the foundation of your dreams. We can be everything God ordained us to be when we start to speak it as though it has already happened. In other words... watch your mouth!! This was something my mom would say to us when we were on the verge of being disrespectful. We had to make sure we did not cross that fine line into disrespect. We knew if she said watch your mouth; you were probably one step away from getting in trouble. It makes me laugh now, but back then it was not funny. I knew exactly what my mom meant when she used that phrase. She was telling us to rethink the words we are about to use to make sure it comes out the right way. I am using this example because I want you to understand just how serious your words are. Be careful of what is coming out of your mouth, because those words will be the determining factor as to where you are going in life. We must choose our words wisely and make sure they match up with our destiny and not our current situation.

Are you ready to use your words to manifest your dreams? What have you been saying out of your mouth that has hindered you from seeing the manifestation of your vision? Let's start today and take account of what we say.

Before I started my own real estate company, I worked as a realtor for another company. During that time, I decided I wanted to build my brand and get my name out there to attract more customers. When I started at that company, I was not the top selling agent. However, I started calling myself The Number One Agent. I literally put this on my business cards, changed my email to this, and even made videos for social media referring to myself as the Number One Agent. I was known as the Number One Agent, and I became the Number One Agent in my company. They promoted me to managing broker, and I became one of the top leaders of my company. It all started with an affirmation I declared over myself. I confessed it daily. I believed it and walked in it. Your words have power, and your words do matter.

YOUR OIL IS VALUABLE

I entitled this chapter ",Your Oil Is Valuable," based on the story in the bible about the widow in 2 Kings Chapter 4:1-7. I encourage you to go back and read the entire story. The story talks about a widow who owed a debt, and the debtor was coming to take her sons to be slaves in order to pay the debt. She asked the prophet Elisha for help and what she should do. In verse 2, Elisha says to the woman, "What can I do to help you?" Elisha asked, "Tell me what do you have in your house?" Nothing at all, except a flask of olive oil," she replied (2 Kings 4:2). The widow thought the one flask of olive oil was nothing. She thought it was not enough to help her in her situation. What she did not realize is a flask of oil was all she needed.

The prophet told her to borrow vessels from her friends and neighbors and go into her house, shut the door behind her, and pour the oil in the vessels. The oil kept flowing until they ran out of vessels. God simply multiplied what she already had in the house. The prophet then told her to sell the oil to pay her debts and use the rest to live off of. He did not tell her to give it away and ask for donations. He told her to sell it because he knew the oil had value. The oil had so much value it would be enough to take care of her debt and enough left for her to live off of.

I want you to know that your oil is valuable. What is your oil? Your oil is the gifts, the talents, and abilities God has placed on the inside of you. Your oil is your special anointing that only you have, and you can only get it from God. What has God anointed you to do? Whatever it is, He did not intend for you to give it away for free. He gave it to you so your gift would make room for you. He gave it to you as a Kingdom Entrepreneur so you could use it to help build the Kingdom and fund Kingdom Projects. Give your gifts, special talents, and abilities to God and let Him multiply them. Remember when the widow went into her home and shut the door behind her? That was when the oil multiplied. What this tells us is that in order for our oil to keep flowing, we must go into the secret place of the Most High to experience His presence. In His presence is where you will see God take what you already have and expand it to levels you never thought you would reach.

So, what can we learn from the widow in this story? There are so many lessons, but I want to examine a few:

1. Obedience

Obedience is key as a believer. Obedience is not something that we only do when we feel like it or we are in the mood to do it. A

Kingdom Entrepreneur's success is solely based on his or her obedience to God. The widow did everything she was told to do and, as a result, she reaped a reward. So, what did we learn? Obedience to God will yield excellent results.

2. What she had was enough

You have everything you need on the inside of you to be successful. I know you may hear this all the time, but it is true. We know God is an intentional God, and when He created you, it was for a purpose. Since He had a purpose in mind, He placed inside of you what you need to fulfill that purpose.

3. You must surrender to God

Stop trying to figure it out and surrender to God. Go to Him and ask for the answers you need. Let Him guide your every move so He can increase you and use you for His Glory. Guess what? We do not always have the answers and that is OK. Let God be your guiding force. He will never steer you wrong.

4. Her Connections were also valuable

The widow had friends and neighbors she could borrow vessels from. These people actually added value to her situation because they were able to help increase her capacity to receive more oil. What value do the people you are connected with bring to you? Are you learning from them? Are you being inspired by them? Are they pushing you towards your dreams or away from them? Our connections should help us to grow and make room for more.

Let's take these valuable lessons we learned from the widow and use them to make sure we value our oil and continue to allow God to fill us up daily until our cups are overflowing with His anointing.

Your gifts are special, and God desires you to share them with the world. Just as God multiplied the widow's oil, He will also multiply you and increase your capacity to do more and accomplish more for the Kingdom. Give God your oil and watch Him take you from faith to faith and Glory to Glory.

I have seen first-hand how God will increase you and take you higher and higher when you allow Him to lead. The good thing about letting God lead is that He knows how far to take you, and His timing is always perfect. Sometimes we get frustrated when we do not see things moving at the rate we want them to, but be content in knowing God knows exactly where you need to be and at what time you should be there.

I look back to where I was when I first began my entrepreneurship journey and where I am today. God increased me tremendously over time. It's been almost 12 years since I first stepped out on faith and I have learned so much about being a business owner since then. The path God chose for me was not an easy one, but it was worth it. I want you to say this prayer over yourself and your business:

Lord, I thank You for the gifts, talents, and abilities You have placed inside of me. Thank You for continuing to grow and increase me every day as I surrender to You. Thank You for choosing me to be a Kingdom Entrepreneur and allowing me to be Your vessel in the marketplace. My goals for my business are aligned with Your Will. Thank You for pouring out fresh oil over me, my family, and my business. I thank You God, that I am a good steward over the gifts You have given me. Thank You, God, for giving me fresh, new, creative, and innovative ideas to grow my business for Your Glory. In Jesus' name, I pray. Amen.

ARE YOU A SERVANT LEADER?

Entrepreneurship and leadership go hand in hand. If you do not want the responsibility of being a leader, then you do not want to be an entrepreneur. Leadership is more than just telling someone what to do. Leadership requires you to show people what to do. Leadership requires you to serve those you lead. Being a servant leader requires you to give of your time, wisdom, and knowledge. It also requires you to put the needs of others above yourself. When the people you lead feel that you genuinely care about them, they will work hard and oftentimes go above and beyond to show their gratitude. As a leader, your goal should be to nurture and develop more leaders. If the people I lead are not growing, then I need to re-evaluate myself as their leader.

Some characteristics of a good leader are as follows:

1. Willing to be transparent to those you lead.

The worst thing you could do as a leader is to not be open and honest with those you lead. A leader must be able to have open and honest communication about concerns within their organization. Even if it is a difficult conversation to have, leaders have to master delivering difficult messages in a positive way. What I mean by that is being aware of your tone and the words you choose to deliver the message.

2. Always be empathetic to the feelings of those you lead.

This was something I had to learn and have gotten better at as time went by. I do not want you to take this as me being someone who does not have empathy for others because I am not. What I am saying is I have learned to be more empathetic to what others consider to be an issue which I may not think is. For example, if you have kids you know some of the things they consider to be emergencies in their world really are not in an adult world. As a parent, because you know the situation will be handled, does not mean you devalue their genuine feelings by saying things that will make them feel like their feelings or concerns do not matter. So, think of this when the people you lead have genuine concerns about something that you as a leader may or may not look at as an issue because you can fix the problem. Be careful and make sure you do not demean them by dismissing their feelings or dismissing the issue as if it does not matter to you.

3. Never ask your team to do something you are not willing to do or have not done.

As I stated before, those you lead are looking for you to show them how to do it and not just tell them. They want you to show them how they can be successful. They also want to feel you know how it feels to be where they are and can be empathetic to what they may go through. As leaders, we have to be to our team what we expect from them.

4. Ask your team what they expect from you.

It is also important for a leader to ask their team members this question: Am I providing what you need as a leader in order for you to grow? Be open to the feedback and be intentional about really listening and receiving.

5. Be willing to sacrifice for your team.

As a leader, we sometimes have to make sacrifices in order to benefit the whole team. When your team sees you are willing to make sacrifices, they, too, will emulate your behavior.

6. As a Kingdom Entrepreneur and leader, you have to stay in consistent prayer with our Heavenly Father.

Remember, in any organization, everything the leader has in them will trickle down throughout their organization. If you carry the anointing, the anointing will trickle down and flow throughout your team. For our oil to flow continuously, we can never forget where our help comes from. Remember this, the oil must flow for us to grow!

10 Practical Tips For An Entrepreneur

1. Never be afraid to stand out.

You have been called to stand out as an entrepreneur. You have been called to lead and show others a path they did not realize was there. You have been called to resolve problems and come up with solutions. If you try to fit in with everyone, you will miss out on reaching the people you have been called to serve in your business. It is the uniqueness about you which will make your business successful. Remember, there is absolutely no one else on this earth like you. Whatever is different about you is your gift from God, so use it and do not be afraid.

2. There are no failures in business, only lessons.

When things do not go as planned, look at what you can learn from the situation. I gained most of my experience and what I know from lessons or things not going the way I planned.

Remember, during this journey, you will have plenty of lessons. The lessons are there to teach you, not to make you quit.

3. Ask for help when you need it.

It's ok to ask for help. Never let pride hinder you from learning what you need to learn or grow in ways you could not possibly orchestrate on your own. When God sends you mentors and other divine vessels to speak into your life, be open to them and listen. Always stay teachable. None of us know everything

4. Get a Mentor.

The quickest way to get to where you want to go is to find someone who is currently doing it or has already achieved it. A mentor can guide you through certain lessons without you having to go through them in your process. When choosing your mentor, ask God for discernment and for Him to send the person He has divinely chosen for you. Remember, as Kingdom Entrepreneurs, we move differently. We consult with our CEO (God) about everything.

5. Read Books.

Read books that will add value and contribute to your personal and spiritual growth. Everyone knows that those who read will always lead.

6. Never be afraid to ask for what is owed to you.

You are worth every penny you charge someone for your products or services. If they could do it themselves, they would not have to come to you. Remember, you are valuable and let no one try to devalue your gifts, talents, and abilities. You are worth it!!!

7. Never Burn Bridges.

The same person you burned a bridge with may be the same person you need to call on in the future for help. The business community is not as big as you may think, and burning bridges in your business community could be detrimental to your business. Learn to always be professional and cordial even when you do not agree with someone. No one is saying you have to be best friends, but you can be cordial. Never vent on social media about situations that happened in business or about your clients. This could be a big turnoff to those watching and they may decide not to do business with you just because of your sharing. Clients or potential business partners do not want to work with someone who may blast every disagreement they could have with you on social media.

8. Network, Network, Network!!!

Like they say, your network is your net worth. I cannot tell you how many times doors were open for me just because I knew someone who had the access to open the door. Network with people in your field and outside of your field. As the saying goes, it is not always what you know, but who you know.

9. Be Open to Change

A Kingdom Entrepreneur is constantly evolving mentally and spiritually. When I say be open to change, ultimately, I am referring to being intentional about your growth. Allowing yourself the opportunity to grow in all areas of your life will have a domino effect on your journey as an entrepreneur. Never get to a place in your life where you think you have arrived. As long as you have breath in your body, you should always seek growth and transformation.

10. Honor Your Word

Mean what you say and say what you mean. Always be clear on what you can and cannot do. You will go far in business when you simply honor your word. If for some reason something happens where you are not able to do what you said, go out of your way to make it right.

I am honored God chose me to be a Kingdom Entrepreneur. I believe if you are reading this book, He chose you, too. We have been called to the marketplace to show the world that you can be a business owner and still profess God in your business. We have been specifically chosen to be trailblazers and be the solution for many of the problems of the world.

This is a prophetic word of wisdom I am literally getting from the Holy Spirit as I am writing this: You cannot quit when things get tough. God placed everything you need inside of you to be successful. There will be times where things will not work out the way you may have planned, but everything will work out the way God planned. Every hardship is a lesson, and every lesson will catapult you to your next level. Keep your spiritual eyes and ears on God to hear His instructions clearly. Make fasting and praying a part of your lifestyle and you will always be one step ahead. Lastly, remember that all you do and accomplish is for the Glory of God.

Prayer for You and Your Business

Dear God, I thank You for the person who has read this book. I thank You for their life and the assignment You have placed on their life. I thank You that they will start to see themselves the way You see them. I thank You for engulfing them with extraordinary grace, favor, and wisdom. I thank You, God, for granting them access to supernatural acceleration as they continue to do Your will while in the marketplace. I thank you God, for constantly equipping them to be a giant in Kingdom Business all for Your Glory. Thank You for Your Everlasting Love and reminding us every day when we wake up that You have a purpose and a plan for our lives. I give You all the Glory, Honor, and praise, in Jesus' name. Amen.

Bonus Just for You

As you all know, real estate is where I got my start in entrepreneurship and then evolved into real estate investing. I truly believe real estate is the key to building wealth. Many have built multi- million-dollar fortunes by owning and investing in real estate. I want to share with you what God gave me to build wealth for me and my family for generations to come. This is a condensed version of my real estate workbook that I still teach from in my "Women Flip Houses, Too" platform and live by in all of my real estate investments.

In order to start a career in real estate investing, there are a few key terms you should know.

REAL ESTATE TERMS TO KNOW

Equity: The difference between the present market value of a property and the amount the owner owes on the property's mortgage. The value of equity builds up gradually over time as the mortgage balance reduces and the property value appreciates.

Cash Flow: Cash Flow refers to the amount of money an investor can pocket at the end of each month after payment of all operating expenses, including loan payments. Cash flow can be positive or negative. If you spend less money than you earn, you will have a positive cash flow. If the cash outflows are more than the cash inflows, you will have a negative cash flow.

ROI (Return on Investment)

Is the most common profitability ratio. There are several ways to determine ROI, but the most frequently used method is to divide net profit by total assets. So, if your net profit is $100,000 and your total assets are $300,000, your ROI would be.33 or 33 percent.

ARV (After Repair Value)

The after repair value is the value of a property after it is improved, renovated, or fixed up. It is the estimated future value of the property after repair. ARV is determined by referencing nearby comparable properties (comps) in similar condition, age, size, build, and style that have recently sold.

Comparables:

A comparable property, also known simply as a "comparable," is used by appraisers to determine the fair market value of a home. Comparables are recently sold properties that have similar sizes, locations and amenities as the property being appraised.

Holding Costs:

Also known as carrying costs. These are the costs associated with owning a piece of real estate during a rehab. These costs may include monthly mortgage payments, insurance, utilities, and security.

Wholesale: A wholesaler contracts a home with a seller, then finds an interested party to buy it. The wholesaler contracts the home with a buyer at a higher price than with the seller and keeps the difference as profit. Real estate wholesalers generally find and contract distressed properties.

Assignment: The transfer of a contract or right from one person to another.

. . .

Assignee: The person to whom something is assigned.

Assignor: The party who makes an assignment.

Now that you have the real estate terms and you understand the real estate language, let's talk about how you can evaluate a deal and determine if it would be a good real estate investment property. When you are looking for a property to flip, there is a simple formula you can use every single time to make sure the numbers work. Typically, we are looking to make at least a 30-35% profit on our real estate deals if they are flips. You can certainly look for less if that is your preference and of course anything above 35% is a bonus. Since you are looking for 35% profit, then the property you choose must be able to be repaired and bought at 65% of the after repair value. As stated above, the after repair value is simply what you can sell the property for after it is repaired.

How Do We Calculate the After Repair Value?

The after repair value is determined by searching for comparable properties that have sold in that neighborhood in the last 6 months or less. The properties you search must be within that same neighborhood or no more than 5 miles from your subject property. The closer you find the comparables to the subject property and the most recently sold comparables will give you the most accurate after repair value. The comparable properties you choose must also have the same number of bedrooms, baths and similar in square footage. The differential in square footage should be no more than 100-200 square feet than the subject property. Once you are able to find 3-5 comparables, you will then take the average and that number is your after repair value. For example, if I find three comparables as follows:

200k+210k+205k=615k

615k/3=205k

205k=ARV

Now that you have your ARV, you can determine if the subject property will be a good deal to flip by taking 65% of the ARV and using that amount to purchase the property and repair it. In this example, 65% of 205k is $133,250.00. If you can acquire the property and complete the repairs for this amount, you would have a good deal on your hands.

What is my Return on Investment (ROI)?

I have spent 133,250 to buy the property and for repairs. I can sell the property for 205,000, so my profit is 71,750. Next, I will divide my profit by my total asset to determine my ROI.

71750/205000=35%

ROI=35%

When you are searching for comparable properties to determine your ARV, you can use any of the free real estate websites online if you do not have access to your local multiple listing system.

Wholesaling

Wholesaling is another form of real estate investing. It has less liability, and it takes little to no money to get started. With wholesaling, your biggest challenge will be finding the properties that you can get under contract. As a wholesaler, you will typically look for distressed properties that sellers want to sell as is. Your primary customer as a wholesaler will be real estate investors who are looking to flip properties. Most investors do not mind paying assignment fees as long as the numbers still work like we discussed with the flip formula. Many wholesalers find their properties through making cold calls, putting out signs and, most importantly, networking with other real estate investors. A wholesaler will find a homeowner who may have a distressed property they want to sell and will place that home under contract with their wholesale company. They will then take the contract and assign it to an investor for a higher amount. The difference between the original contract and what the wholesaler assigned the contract for is the wholesaler's assignment fee. For example:

Wholesaler Mindy has gotten homeowner Jane's home under contract for 70k. Jane's property is distressed, and she wants to sell it as is. The wholesaler then reassigns the contract to investor Kim for 80k. The wholesaler makes a 10k profit; the homeowner gets 70k, and the investor gets the property. Wholesaling is a great way to build up your capital to get started in flipping homes, too. Please be mindful that in some states a license is required for wholesaling, but not in most. Before you start, check your particular state to make sure you do not need a license.

All of these techniques are taught in more detail through our Women Flip Houses, Too Platform.

About the Author

Danita Hayes is the wife of Chris Hayes Sr. and mother of three children, Nadia, Nia and Chris Hayes, Jr.. She is a *Kingdom Entrepreneur* and owns a diverse portfolio of businesses. Danita began her entrepreneurship journey as a real estate broker and today co-owns a real estate firm that has two branch offices. She also co-owns a cafe that has two locations and several real estate investment companies. Danita recently started a movement called "*Women Flip Houses, Too*", which was created to teach women all over the world how to invest in real estate and build wealth for their families.The *Women Flip Houses, Too* movement has allowed Danita to pour into thousands of women and give them the tools to be successful real estate investors. Danita is passionate about inspiring women to execute their vision through focusing on God first and allowing Him to work through them to accomplish their goals. She also created the *21 Days of Encouragement* interactive journal for women entrepreneurs to encourage and guide women to reach their entrepreneurial goals. Danita uses Matthew 6:33 as the blueprint on how she lives her life: "Seek Ye first the Kingdom of God and all of His righteousness and all these things will be added unto you."

Made in United States
Orlando, FL
04 March 2023

30675146R00070